The Cover
Embossed Design after
Harry Jackson's
Cowboy Meditation, 1964

Harry Jackson:
A Retrospective Exhibition

Text by
Gene Thornton

Buffalo Bill
Historical Center

Cody, Wyoming

Participating Museums

Buffalo Bill Historical Center
Cody, Wyoming

Palm Springs Desert Museum
Palm Springs, California

Minneapolis Institute of Arts
Minneapolis, Minnesota

Copyright 1981 Buffalo Bill Historical Center

All rights reserved. Except for use in a review, the reproduction or utilization of this work in any form or by an electronic, mechanical, or other means, now known or hereafter invented, including xerography, photocopying, and recording, and in any information storage and retrieval system is forbidden without the written permission of the publisher.

Library of Congress Catalogue Card Number: 81-66495

I.S.B.N. Number 0-931-618-04-5

Contents

Preface   6

Harry Jackson:
A View from New York   7

The Paintings   10

The Bronzes   30

Checklist   68

Selected Bibliography   70

Preface

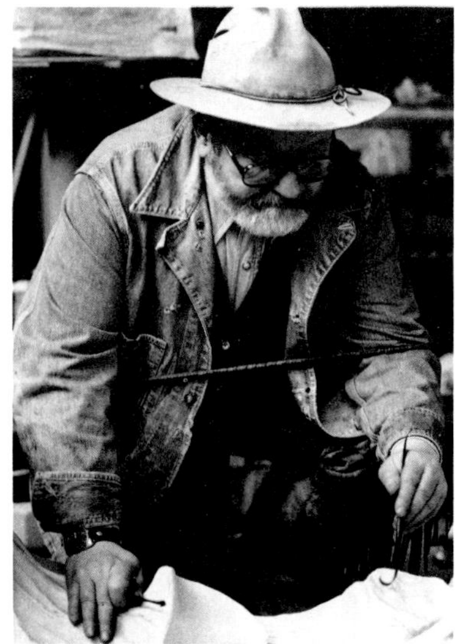

Harry Jackson in his Camaiore Italy Studio 1980.

With his feet planted firmly on the clay splattered floor of his Italian studio and his heart and mind fixed devotedly on the Far West, Harry Jackson bridges time and space in a way remarkable for an American artist of today. His vision and experience are at once worldly and regional, thereby bringing to his western subjects a cool sophistication and warm human empathy. The dichotomy has proven a rich staple in the nourishment of an extraordinary artistic talent.

In 1958 the Honorable Robert D. Coe commissioned Harry Jackson to complete two mural sized paintings portraying the rugged life on the western plains. These two canvases, *The Stampede* and *The Range Burial,* were intended to find a permanent home in the Whitney Gallery of Western Art and would come to Cody as a gift of the W.R. Coe Foundation. Along with two companion sculptural studies of these same subjects, which resulted from the commission, the paintings were displayed in the Whitney Gallery in the early 1960's and portended the significant commitment which the Museum would have in subsequent years to contemporary, as well as historic, western art.

Those four works also represented an important turning point for Harry Jackson. It had been but a few years since he had abandoned a fruitful decade of abstract expressionist painting and returned to the figurative tradition. Now, with these new monumental works, he was able to contemplate the great West, a theme and a place which had long held a grasp on the man and his life force. Since that time, Jackson's career has demonstrated a conscious and sustained effort to transform the substance of western life into the language of art. And, his move into sculpture, a result of his studies for the two monumental paintings, has brought him to the forefront of American artists over the past twenty years.

To embark on plans in 1978 for the organization of a major retrospective exhibition of Jackson's work was therefore a great pleasure and honor for Historical Center personnel. We were encouraged in our scheme by the late Frederick Sleight, then Director of The Palm Springs Desert Museum, who joined early in our efforts. More recently, Samuel Sachs of The Minneapolis Institute of Arts has shared our enthusiasm for a retrospective. Along with the Historical Center, these two institutions will serve as hosts for the exhibition.

Peter H. Hassrick
Director

Buffalo Bill Historical Center

Harry Jackson:
A View from
New York

For many people who know and love Harry Jackson's Western bronzes, the surprise of this retrospective exhibition will be the abstract paintings that he did as a young man, before he turned (or returned) to the West for subject matter. But to those of us who live in New York — and whether you like it or not, New York is the art capital of America, if not of the world — the surprising thing is that Harry Jackson is having any kind of retrospective exhibition at all.

"Harry Jackson? Oh yes, he's that cowboy artist, isn't he?" That is the typical response in the New York art world when his name is mentioned — condemnation by association with a type of subject matter that is not well thought of in New York. More knowledgeable members of the New York art world, those who remember Harry Jackson when he lived and worked here, condemn him more subtly. "Oh yes, Harry Jackson. Back in the early 50's he was a very promising member of the second generation of the Abstract Expressionists. Then he sold out to make that cowboy art. Where did you say his retrospective is — the Buffalo Bill Historical Center in Cody, Wyoming? Well, it figures."

That is what you hear in New York when Harry Jackson's name is brought up in informal conversation. On a more formal level, on the level of published criticism and art history, you hear even less. True, there have been a few newspaper stories about Harry Jackson the man (as opposed to his work) — stories about a portrait commission in Chile, some sort of brouhaha about Cézanne drawings. There was also that picture essay in *Life* magazine how many years ago? — 25? — when *Life* had not yet come out foursquare for modern art. And of course there was the week, 12 years ago, when Harry Jackson's statue of John Wayne was featured on the cover of *Time*.

This kind of personal publicity has increased in the past year or so as news of the truly extraordinary demand for Jackson's Western bronzes has penetrated even into the editorial offices of New York and London art magazines and newspapers. Now we are reading stories of his private foundry in Italy, of his business headquarters in New York, of his jet-lag life between Italy, New York and Wyoming, and how much money he makes — a subject guaranteed to warm any editor's heart. But the few art writers who have come even this far have been wary of writing about his work. The boldest among them ventured to dismiss it as kitsch, cliché, stilted and inept. But most art writers settle for giving him space to speak for himself. They do not try to evaluate his work themselves or to place him in the larger world of art. So far as serious criticism is concerned, he does not exist.

In a way, this does not matter. Harry Jackson has found his public, and once an artist has done this, he does not need the enormous engine of publicity, promotion and salesmanship that is such an important part of the New York art world. In another way, however, it matters very much. Art history is written in New York and in the universities around the country whose artists and art historians look to New York for guidance and approval, and although New York is a cosmopolitan city, it is also in certain ways strangely provincial. Harry Jackson is one of the best loved and most popular of living American artists. He is also a figure of considerable historical importance, a pioneer (though this has not yet been recognized) of the return to realism in painting and sculpture which is now acknowledged, even in New York, as one of the most significant art movements of the past decade in

America. And yet, as far as the New York art world is concerned, he does not exist. There is obviously another art world out there that operates on different principles — a Sunbelt art world, say, that stretches from Palm Beach through Texas and Oklahoma to California, with Snowbelt outposts in Colorado and Wyoming. There is obviously also something lacking in the New York art world that enables it to search all over America for what is significant in American art and not find Harry Jackson.

I well remember a luncheon I attended in 1969 when I was briefly writing art news for *Time* magazine. All the *Time* art staff was there — the senior editor, the two art writers with the rank of contributing editor, and several researchers — and the guest of honor was Henry Geldzahler, now Commissioner of the Department of Cultural Affairs of the City of New York, then Curator of Twentieth Century Art at New York's Metropolitan Museum of Art. *Time* was planning to run a big story on the Metropolitan Museum's 100th anniversary celebration, and so far as the New York art world was concerned, the centerpiece of the celebration was an exhibition of post-war American painting and sculpture officially known as "New York Painting and Sculpture — 1940-1970," but always referred to by everyone in the art world as "Henry's show." The keynote of Henry's show, as he explained it to us, was "pluralism" — that is, the acceptance of different styles of art as equally valid. We all understood what this meant. During the 1950's the only art that had been accepted as properly avant-garde in New York City was Abstract Expressionism, but in the 1960's Pop Art had arrived, and Henry's show would include Andy Warhol as well as Jackson Pollock. That was what "pluralism" meant and nothing more, but as Henry explained it, it sounded like it might mean more, so I asked, "Does pluralism include Harry

Jackson?" There was a brief embarrassed silence from which Henry and I were rescued by a researcher's sensible question, and Harry Jackson was never mentioned again.

No doubt one reason why the New York art world is blind to Harry Jackson is because he so seldom exhibits in New York. In New York as elsewhere, the business of art critics is to review exhibitions, and if artists do not exhibit here, it is hard for our critics to write about them. Harry Jackson has managed to survive, and indeed to flourish, without many New York shows, and so in a way he has only himself to blame.

There is, however, more to it than that, for even when Harry Jackson does exhibit in New York he is usually ignored. It is not because he shows in obscure little galleries (his principal New York shows during the past 20 years were at M. Knoedler & Co. and Kennedy Galleries) or because his work lacks merit — artists of far less merit are reviewed regularly and at length. It is, or so some observers maintain, because he is regarded in the New York art world as a traitor to the cause.

Back in the 1950's when he was a promising second generation abstract expressionist painter, Abstract Expressionism was not just another ephemeral art movement, it was New York's white hope to achieve international leadership in the art world. It was, its supporters said, the first art movement of world-wide significance to originate in America. (People who said this conveniently overlooked how much it owed to European modernism.) It was also the artistic basis (as opposed to the merely commercial basis) for New York's claim to have

replaced Paris as the art capital of the world. Last but not least, it was supposed to last forever. Yet Harry Jackson turned against it — not in the 1960's when the advent of Pop Art suddenly made it seem old-fashioned, but early in the 1950's, when it was still riding high, and not for something with Pop Art's shock appeal, but for something that seemed old-fashioned and sentimental. The cause survived his defection. Abstract Expressionism had its decade of glory, and by the time it had to move over and make room for Pop, New York was firmly established as the art capital of the world. But Harry Jackson was not forgiven, and when the historians began to write the history of American art in the 50's, they simply left him out.

No doubt there is something to this explanation. Harry Jackson did give up abstraction, and historians of Abstract Expressionism did leave him out, or so close to out as not to make any difference. And yet this is not the whole story. Since the 1950's, realism has given abstraction a lot of competition, returning first in the form of Pop Art and Photo Realism, now in the form of an as-yet unnamed back-to-nature realism characterized by meticulously rendered representations done directly from nature. When to these new forms of realism — the last one not so new — are added other new developments of the past two decades such as Op Art, Conceptual Art, Earthworks and Funk Art, it is clear that "pluralism" has carried the day to a degree undreamed of by Henry Geldzahler in 1969, and yet Harry

Jackson is still excluded. Why? Artists like Alfred Leslie, Jack Beal, Philip Pearlstein and Alex Katz, all of whom have their roots in Abstract Expressionism, have made the transition to realism without ever losing the interest of curators and critics, and a younger generation of Back-to-Nature Realists including Catherine Murphy and Rackstraw Downes are praised to the skies.

Is Harry Jackson neglected because he turned to realism too early and so could not conveniently be treated as part of a movement? Possibly. However, a more likely explanation lies in the fact that he returned not just to nature but to the Old Masters, and not just to the Old Masters but (the unforgivable sin against Modernism) to the idea that distinguishes the art of the Old Masters from the art of the Modernists, the idea that art exists not for its own sake or even for the sake of shocking mankind, but for the sake of expressing mankind's hopes and fears. Harry Jackson had taken from Abstract Expressionism the one thing it had to offer a young painter of his generation, an awareness of the formal values of art.

He then discovered what anyone with two eyes and a brain can plainly see; that the Old Masters, beyond whom the Modernists are supposed to have advanced, already knew all about formal values, and knew how to draw as well. It was then that he began the series of paintings from life that culminated in *The Italian Bar,* a painting whose pivotal place in the history of 20th century American art has yet to be recognized. He had not yet rediscovered the subject that had attracted him as a boy — the West — but he had recovered for modern American painting something that it had lost under the onslaught of European Modernism. He had recovered its heart.

"Heart" is not a common term in art criticism, but everyone knows what it means. It means that the artist has succeeded in expressing in his work something that means a lot not just to him but to hundreds and thousands of his fellow human beings. "Heart" is a quality that distinguishes most of the great art of the past up to about the end of the 19th century. It is also the quality that separates the work of Harry Jackson from that of most of the other second generation Abstract Expressionists who have turned to realism since the 1950's. There is something cold and mechanical about their work, something that smacks of Pop Art and Photo Realism. There is an elaboration and stylization of finish over every inch of the picture surface that their elders would have damned as "rendering." There is a lack of interest in subject matter except insofar as it serves as an occasion for a virtuoso demonstration of technique. They are, in a sense, still abstract artists — abstract but not expressionist — even though they are working in a realist convention. Philip Pearlstein is reported to have said that he would rather paint stones than human beings, but stones are heavy and hard to move in and out of the studio, while human beings move in and out by themselves. Even Alfred Leslie, with his complex subject pictures carefully constructed on Old Master principles, seems to be making a demonstration of how traditional techniques can be adapted to modern subjects, rather than using technique to say something meaningful about the subject itself.

Harry Jackson, however, is notoriously interested in his subjects, and this leaves commentators in a peculiar position. There is nothing they can say about his work that the work itself does not say better. There is always plenty to say about a blank canvas, or a canvas covered with blobs and dribbles of paint, or a stuffed goat with an automobile tire around its middle, or a canvas on which chevrons, stripes or circles have been stenciled, or a crushed automobile, or a canvas on which a comic strip or a photograph has been painstakingly copied by hand, or a life-size painted polyvinyl cast of a tired cleaning woman so detailed and realistic that the casual gallery goer mistakes it for a real person. Such art requires explanation. But Harry Jackson's art speaks for itself, leaving commentators with nothing to do but go on to something else.

There are, however, one or two things that can be said about Harry Jackson's art that may make it more intelligible to New Yorkers and to New York-minded people wherever they live. One concerns his relationship to Abstract Expressionism. Like Philip Pearlstein and Alex Katz, Harry Jackson did not reject Abstract Expressionism so much as incorporate its lessons into his mature work. This is perhaps more apparent in his early bronzes, with their rough, unfinished surfaces and lack of color, than in his later ones, which are more detailed and often polychromed, but it is true of the later one, too. "Gestural" is a word often used to describe the swinging abstract design that is common to the realist painting of, say, Pearlstein, and the abstract paintings of some of the older men who were his masters. Could any realist art be more gestural than the art that produced Harry Jackson's *Two Champs?*

Another thing worth saying about Harry Jackson concerns his use of the West as subject matter. When Harry Jackson discovered the American West he discovered a subject that was not just regional or even American but one of the few subjects available to modern artists that is truly international in its appeal. Cowboy movies have made the myth of the American West as familiar to people in Prague and Tokyo as it is to people in Dallas or Cheyenne, and what Harry Jackson has done is give that myth a more permanent expression in painted canvas and bronze.

It is not hard to understand why this myth should be so appealing in an age of closing frontiers and growing restrictions on freedom. It is a myth of unlimited freedom and endless expansion. For more than 200 years, since the great political and industrial revolutions, our civilization has lived by this myth, and for most of those 200 years the myth seemed to be confirmed by reality. Starting, however, with the closing of the frontier in the late 19th century, reality began to undermine the myth, and after two world wars and the end of colonialism, only a handful of newly-rich billionaires still mistake it for reality.

The myth, however, continues to haunt our dreams. Western art of Harry Jackson's sort began in the 19th century as reportage. To city-dwelling Easterners and Europeans, the West was inherently a romantic subject, a far-away place where none of the irksome restraints of city life were felt, yet it was portrayed by the early Western artists, most of whom were reporters and

illustrators, with the same kind of factual detail that other artist-reporters brought to contemporary city life. After the frontier was closed, however, the West as depicted by artists became a landscape of romance. The precise details of everyday life were blurred, and out of the mists of the very recent past archetypal figures began to emerge — the cowboy, the Indian, the sheriff, the outlaw, the settler — who, though based on reality, rose above it to enact a drama of our dreams.

The iconography of this popular art is as familiar and understandable to the modern city dweller as the iconography of medieval church art was to the average Christian of the Middle Ages or the iconography of Renaissance classicism was to the educated Italian townspeople for whom it was created, and in Harry Jackson's work it is treated with a melancholy realism that is wholly of our time. The subject of his first great Western works, *Stampede* and *Range Burial,* is death, and I doubt that anyone who has ever experienced the death of someone he loves can look upon these two works without feeling. The figure of the young cowboy being dragged to his death is perhaps more moving in the sculpted version, where the arm is flung protectively over his face, suggesting that he still hopes to live. But all the versions and fragments of both works are suffused with a sense of loss that distinguishes Jackson's work from that of, say, the turn-of-the-century painter and sculptor, Fredric Remington. In Remington's day the closing of the frontier was still too recent, the battles fought to achieve it still too painfully remembered, for the sense of loss to dominate his art. In our time, however, we have a better idea what was lost when the West was won, not just by the Indians but by their conquerers as well. Though Harry Jackson has never dealt directly with this theme, even such energetic pieces as *Pony*

Express are touched with its melancholy. Study the faces of figures as diverse as Sacagawea, the Gunsil and John Wayne as Rooster Cogburn. They are all contemplating the death of something that is, or should be, dear to us all.

I would like to say something in closing about Harry Jackson's influence on a younger generation of realist painters now emerging in New York — an influence achieved in the best and most traditional way, not through the media but by frequent and direct contact with the artist's actual work. For many years Harry Jackson's first great realist painting, *The Italian Bar,* hung in New York's Little Italy on a wall of the Mare Chiaro Restaurant, the bar it depicts, and for some of those years a group of young painters and sculptors associated with the New York Alliance of Figurative Artists went to that bar on Friday nights after their weekly meeting to relax and talk. These were artists who were trying to find a contemporary way out of the byways of abstraction onto the main road of representational art that stretches back to the ancient Egyptians and forward, we all hope, as far into the future as men and women shall inhabit this earth. During those years, or so I have been told by one of these artists, *The Italian Bar* served as a reminder that serious figurative art was still possible in our time and as an example of how it could be done. The impact of this painting on these young artists was primarily a professional one, but Harry Jackson's Western art can help us all as we try to come to terms with the realities of life and death in our time.

© Gene Thornton 1981

The Paintings

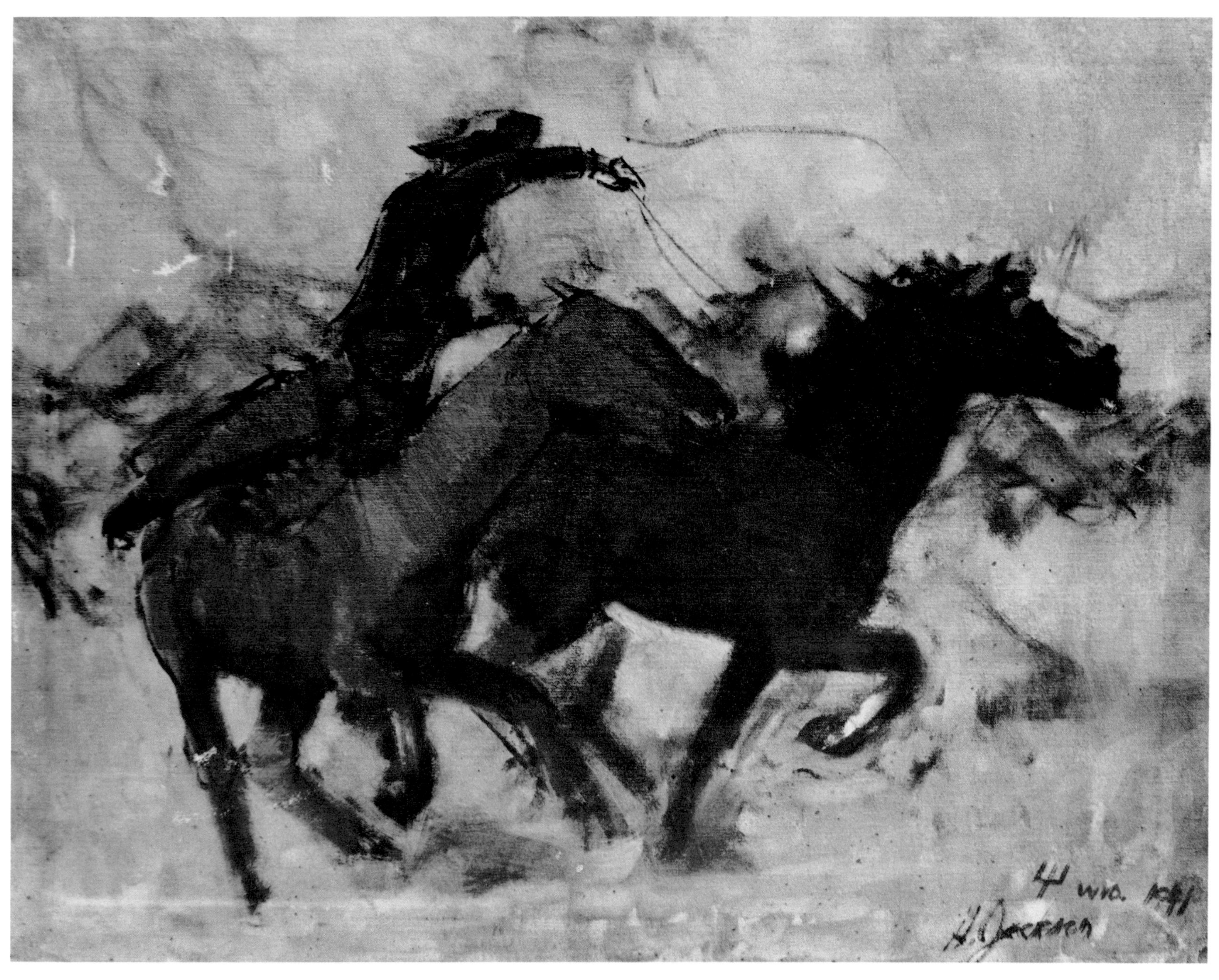

Untitled — cowboy roping horses,
oil on canvas, 24 x 30″, 1941
Wyoming Foundry Studios

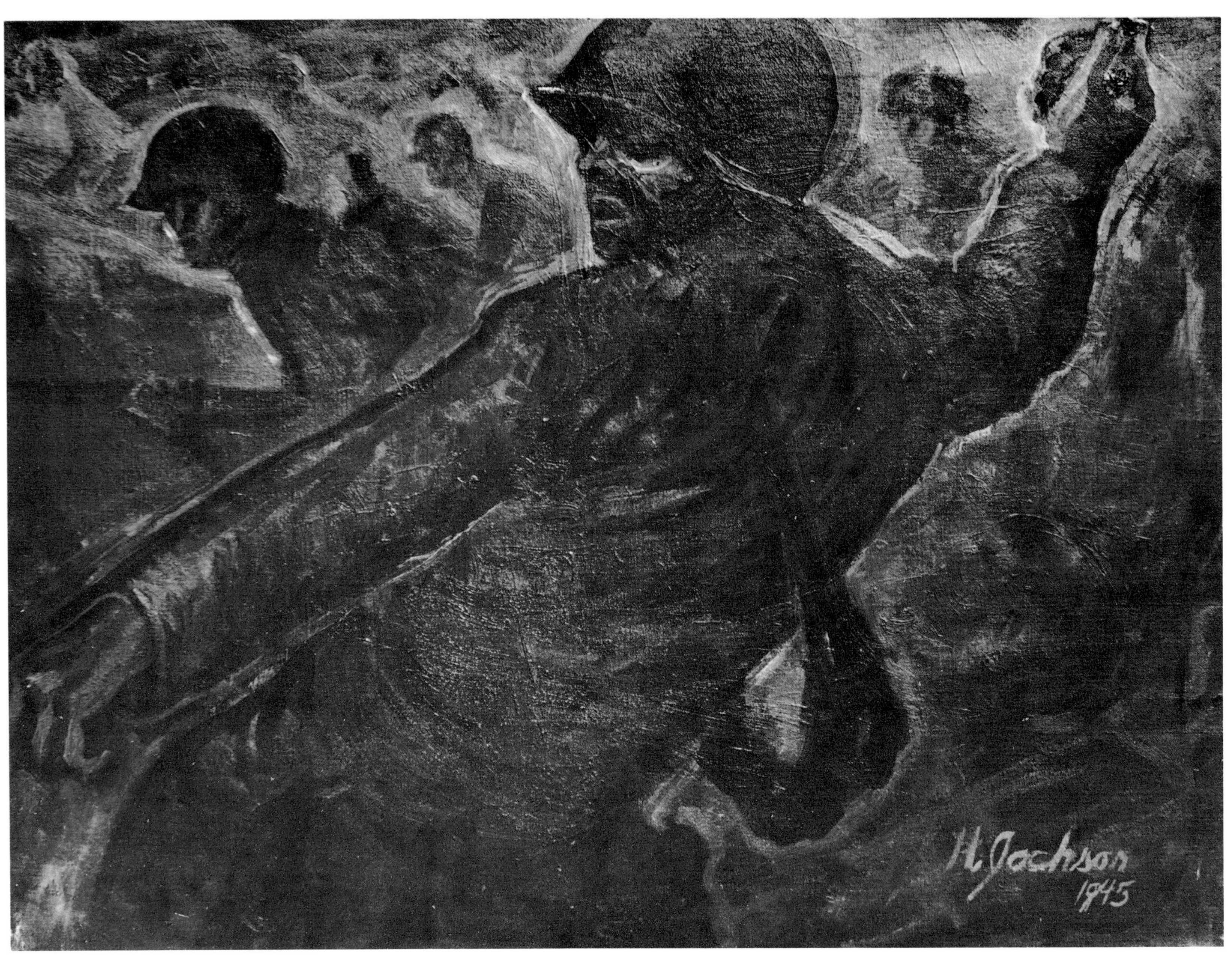

Assault, oil on canvas,
20 x 26″, 1945
Wyoming Foundry Studios

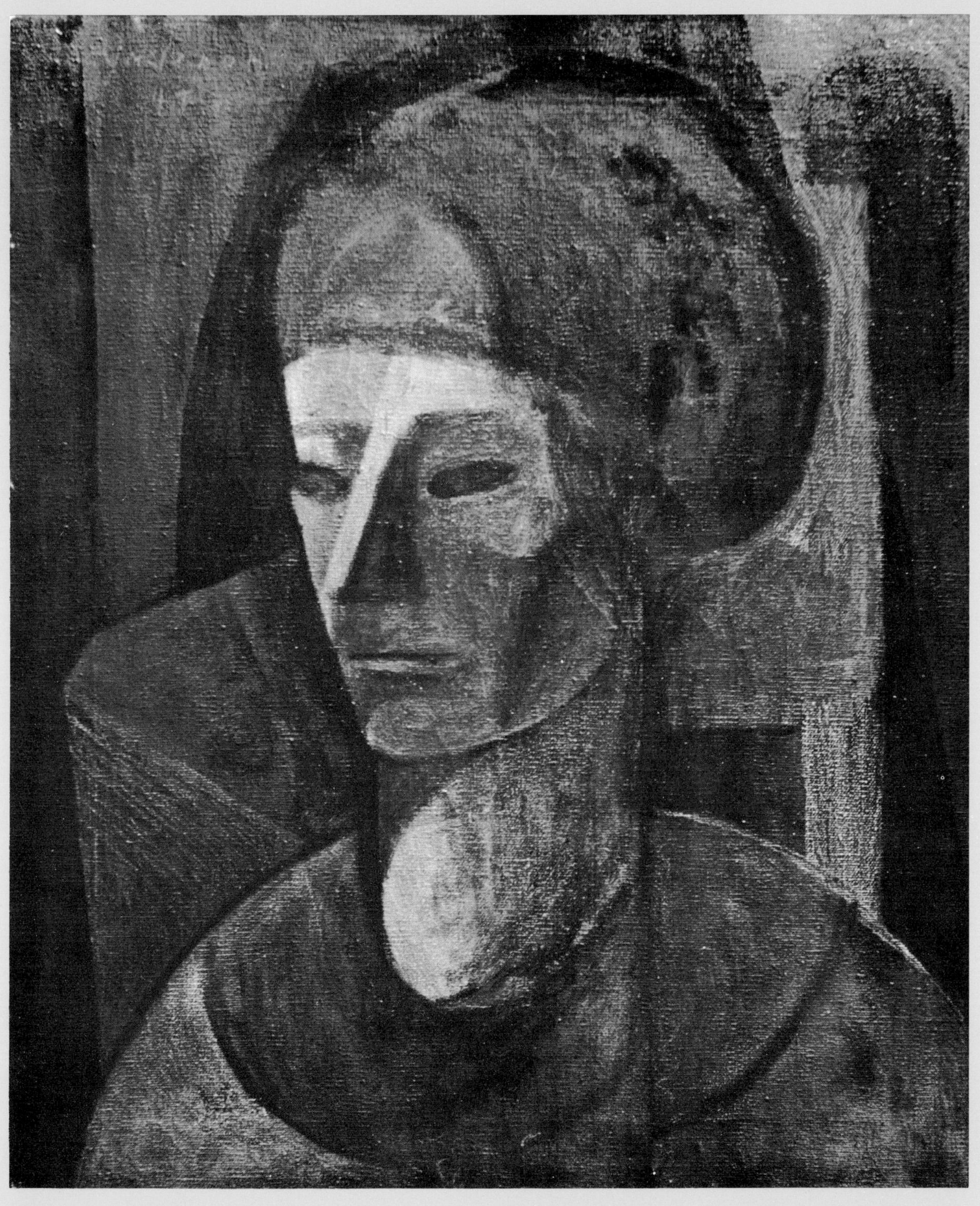

Untitled — portrait bust of
woman, oil on canvas,
22 x 18″, 1947
Wyoming Foundry Studios

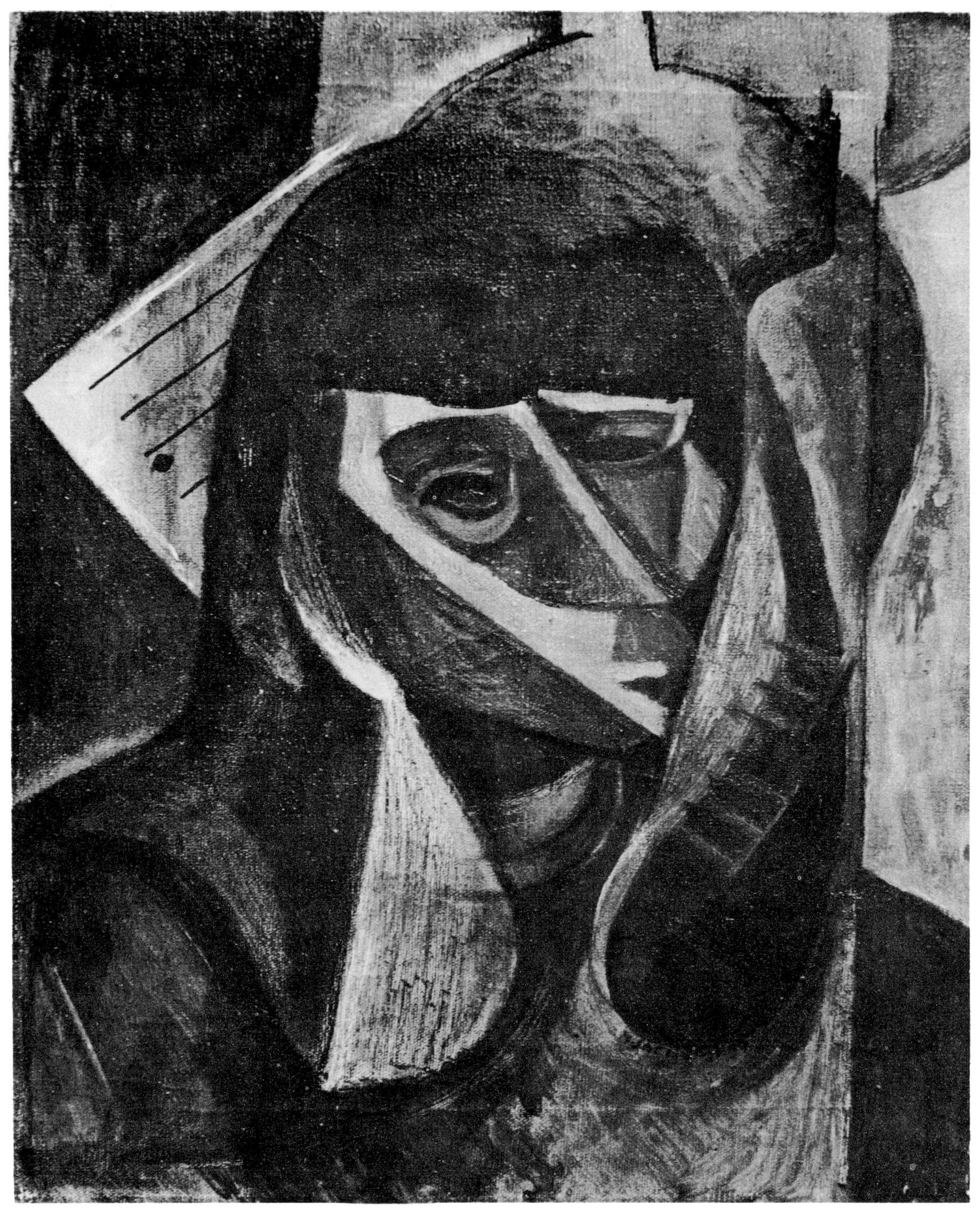

Untitled — portrait bust of
woman, oil on canvas,
20 x 16", 1946
Wyoming Foundry Studios

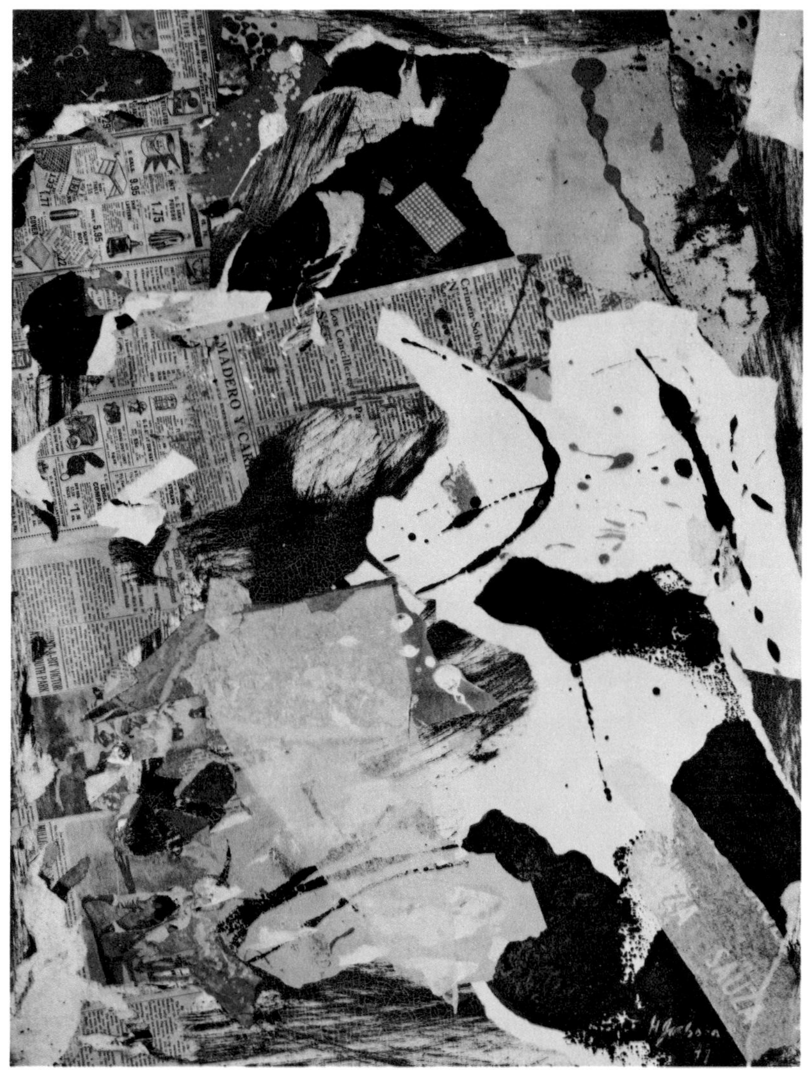

Collage, mixed media,
33 x 24″, 1949
Wyoming Foundry Studios

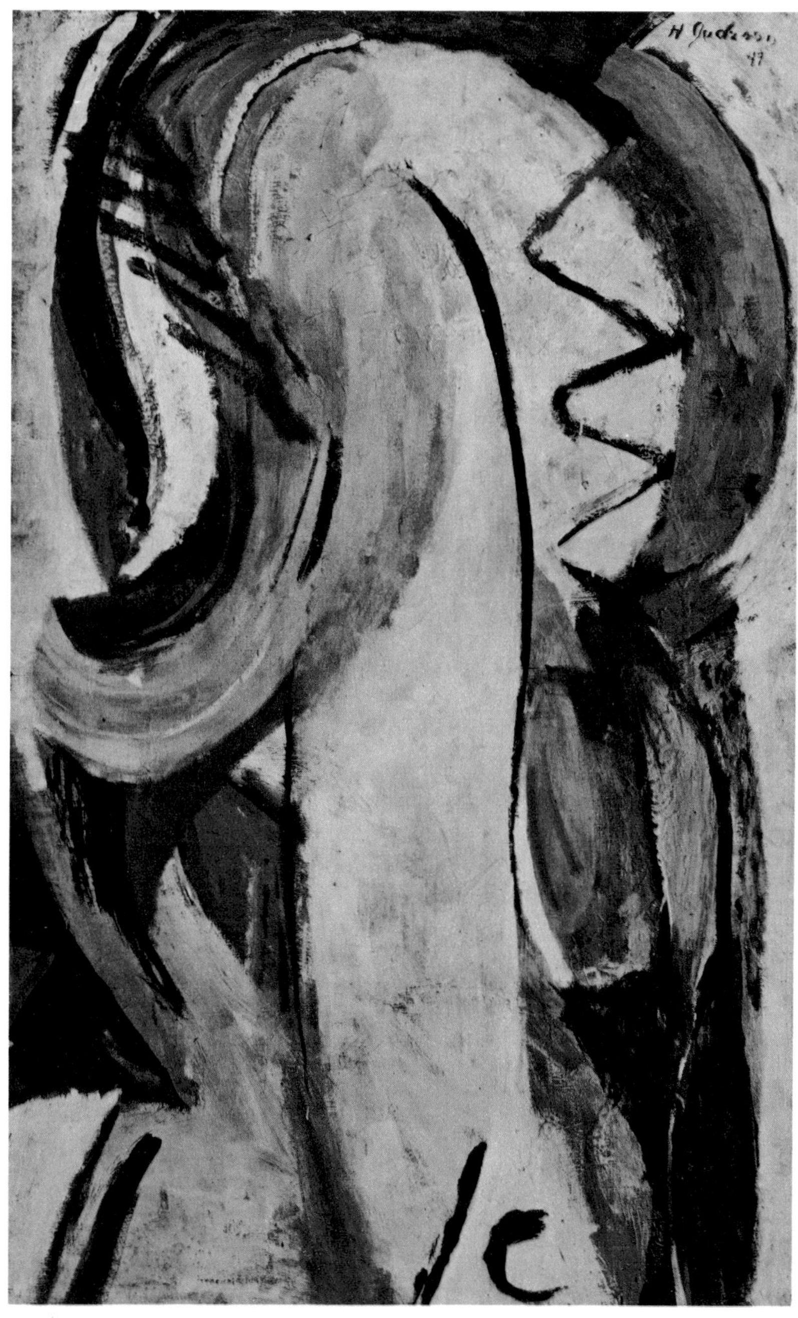

Grace Hartigan, oil on canvas,
36 x 60″, 1949
Wyoming Foundry Studios

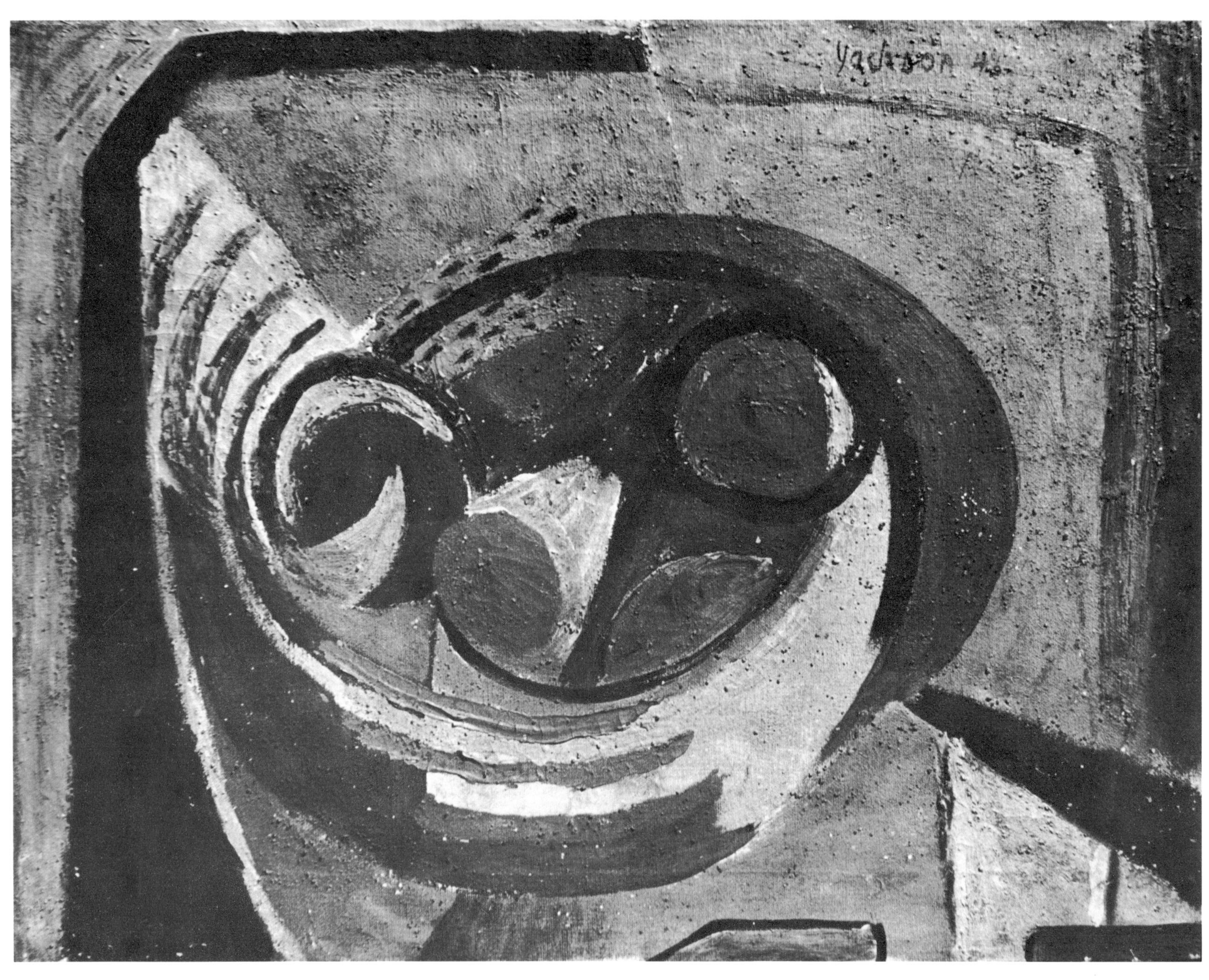

Still Life, oil on canvas,
12 x 16″, 1948
Wyoming Foundry Studios

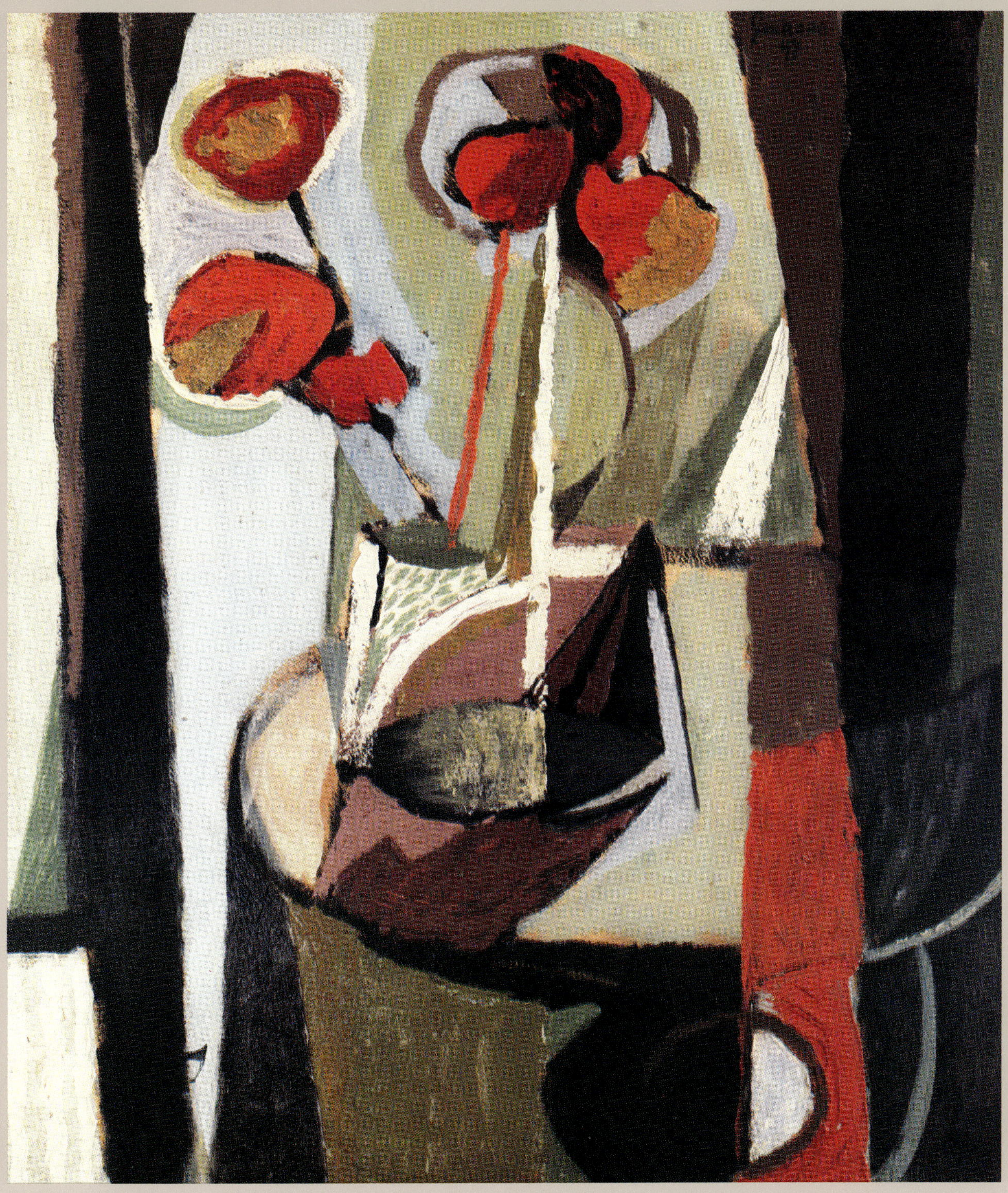

Untitled — Cubist still life,
oil on board,
30¼ x 25″, c. 1947
Wyoming Foundry Studios

Harry Jackson belonged to the avant-garde. He was a pupil of Hans Hofmann, a friend of Jackson Pollock, and was at one time married to Grace Hartigan. His abstract paintings received the highest praise. He was a significant part of a movement which became fashionable to the exclusion of every other style.

Dr. John Walker in
Harry Jackson, 1981

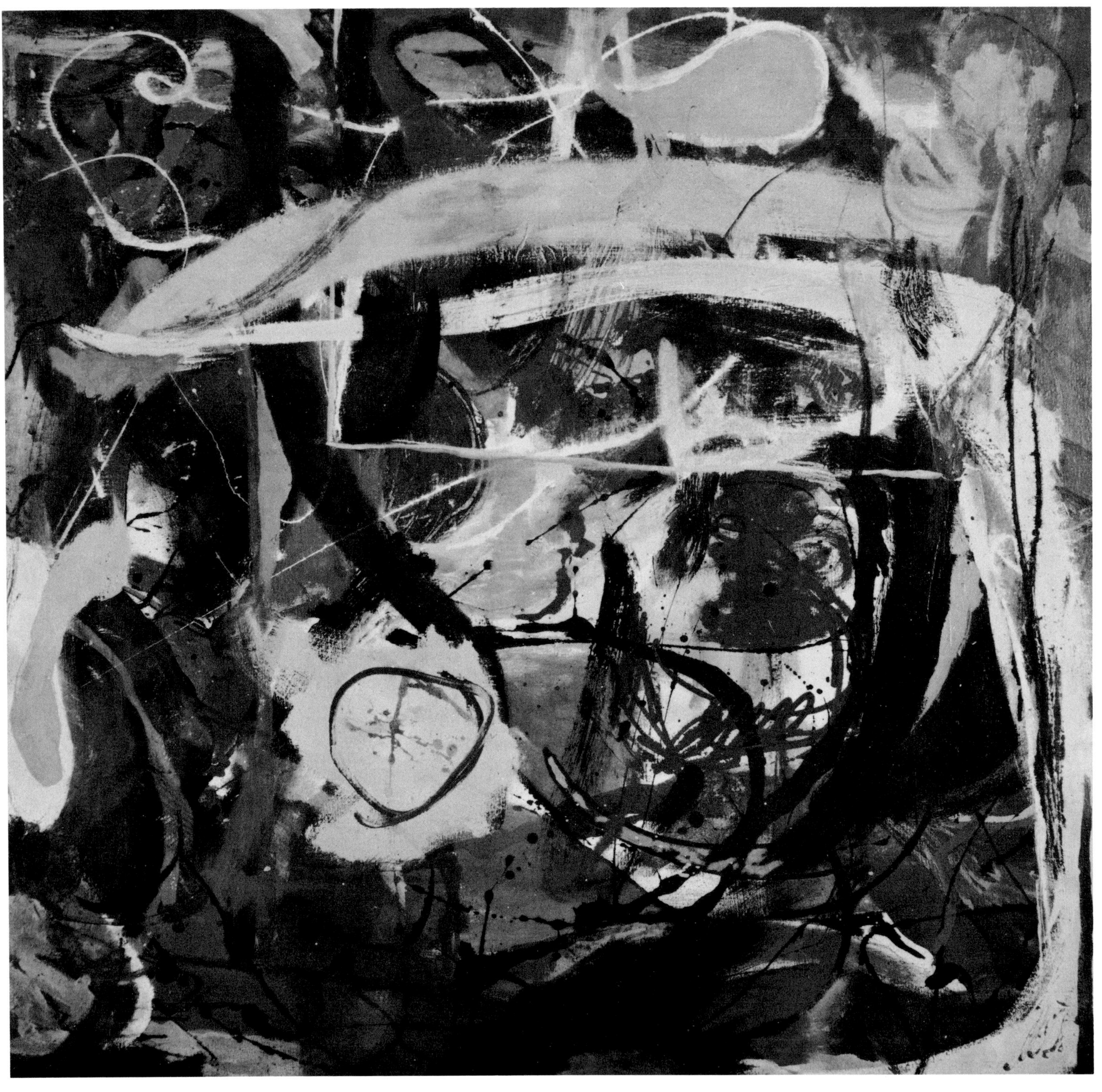

Fiesta, oil on canvas,
40 x 40″, 1950
Dr. Emmanuel Ghent

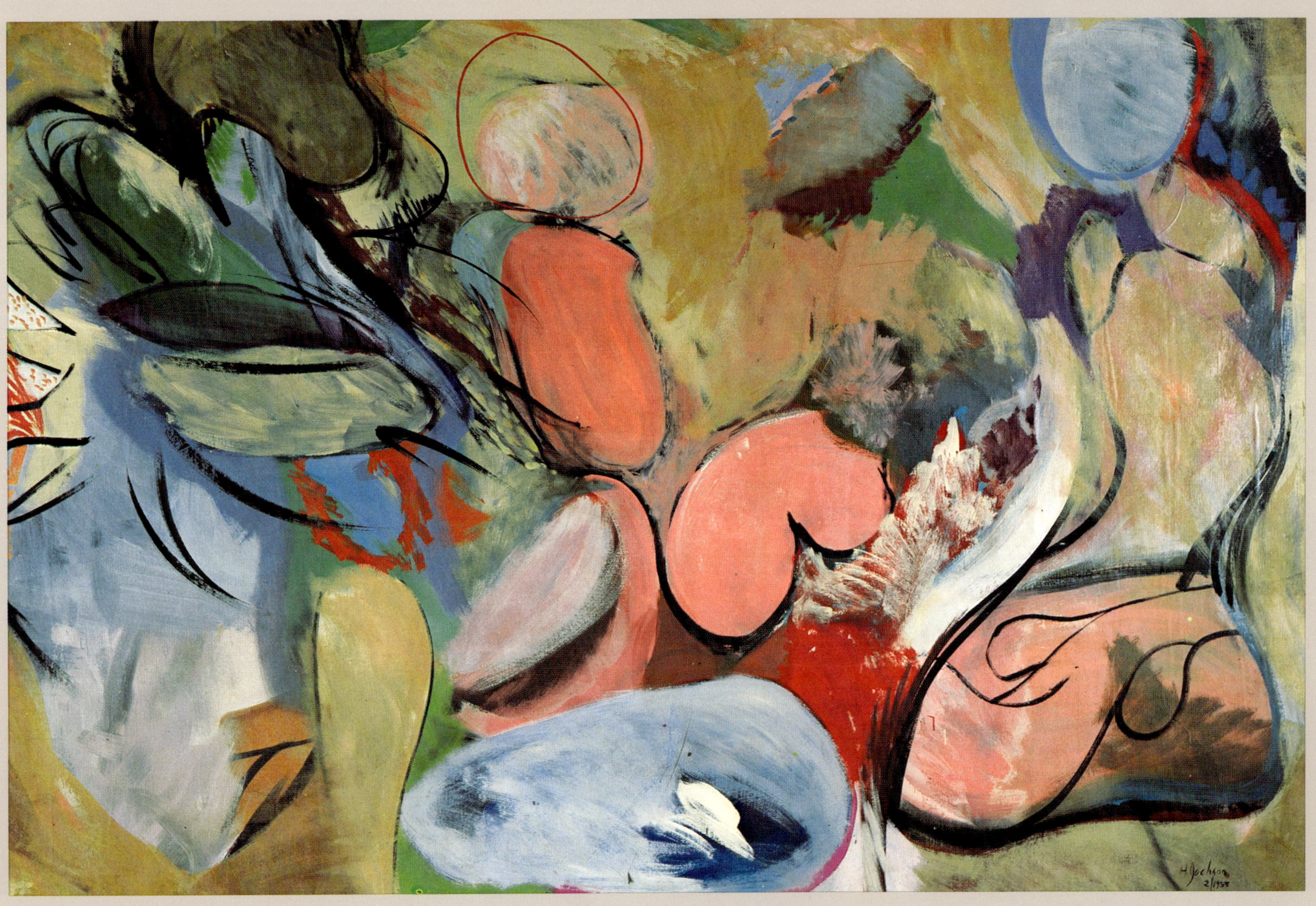

Family, oil on canvas,
92½ x 134″, 1953
Wyoming Foundry Studios

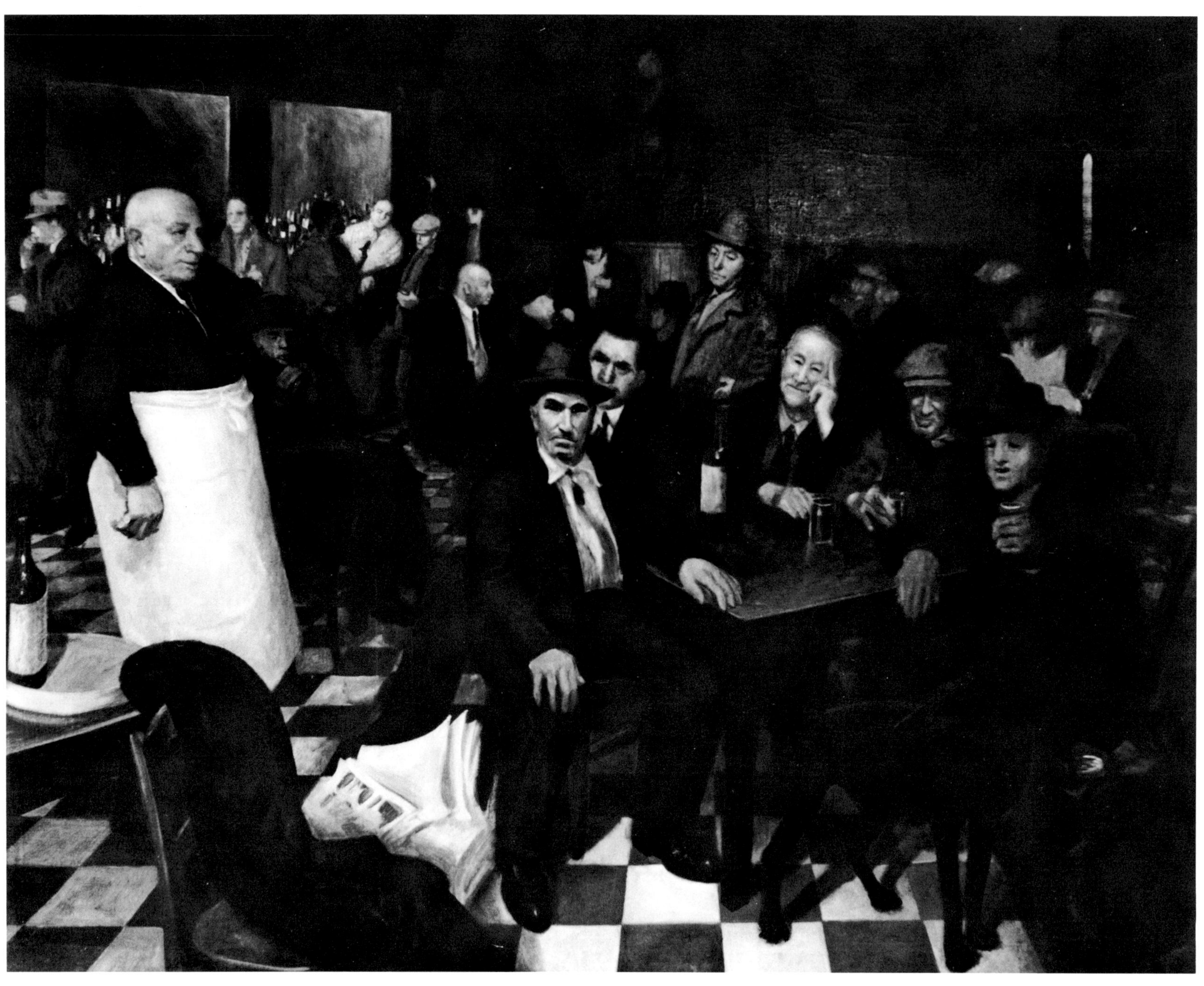

The Italian Bar, oil on canvas,
7 x 9′, 1956
Wyoming Foundry Studios

The Italian Bar is not simply a
casual genre scene . . . It is rather
the apprehension of a way of life in
which every aspect of appearance
has been turned inside out to reveal
the inner life of the social group.
Larry Pointer & Donald Goddard

Harry Jackson, 1981

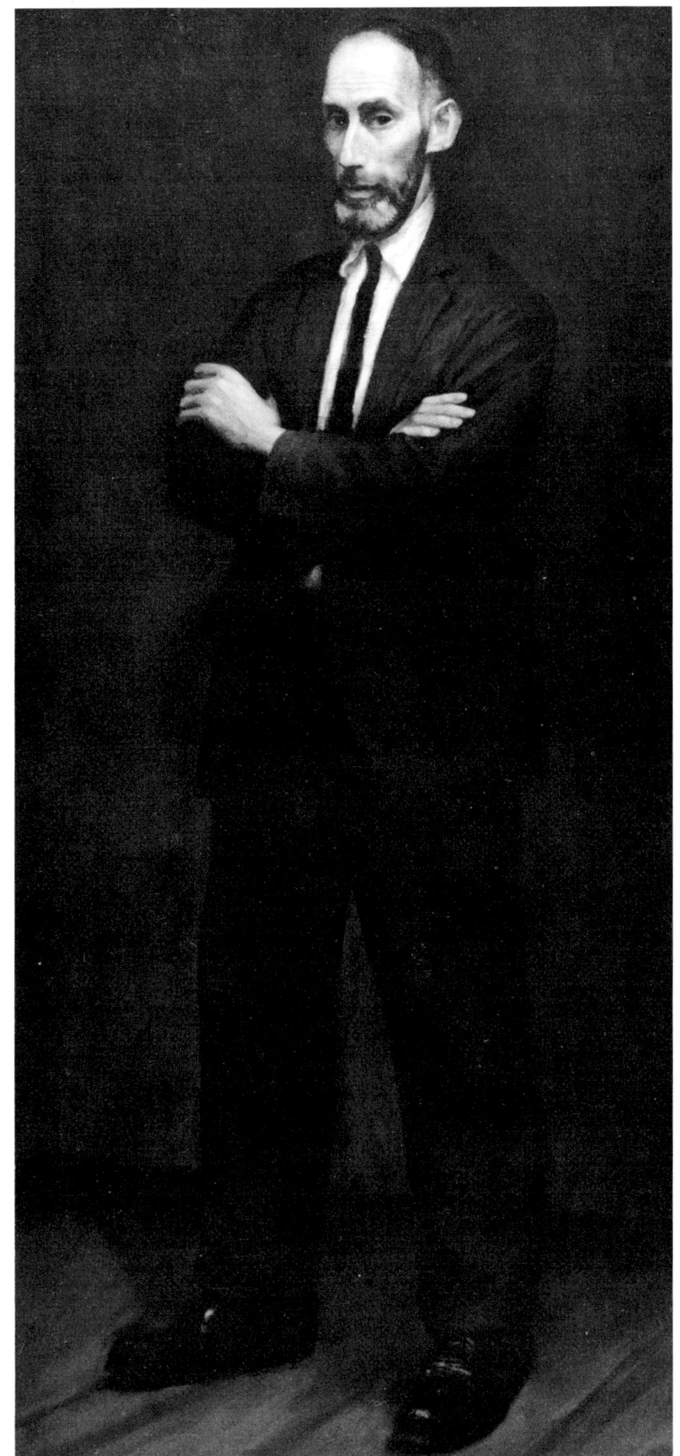

The Poet, Robert Lax,
oil on canvas,
78½ x 35½", 1962
Wyoming Foundry Studios

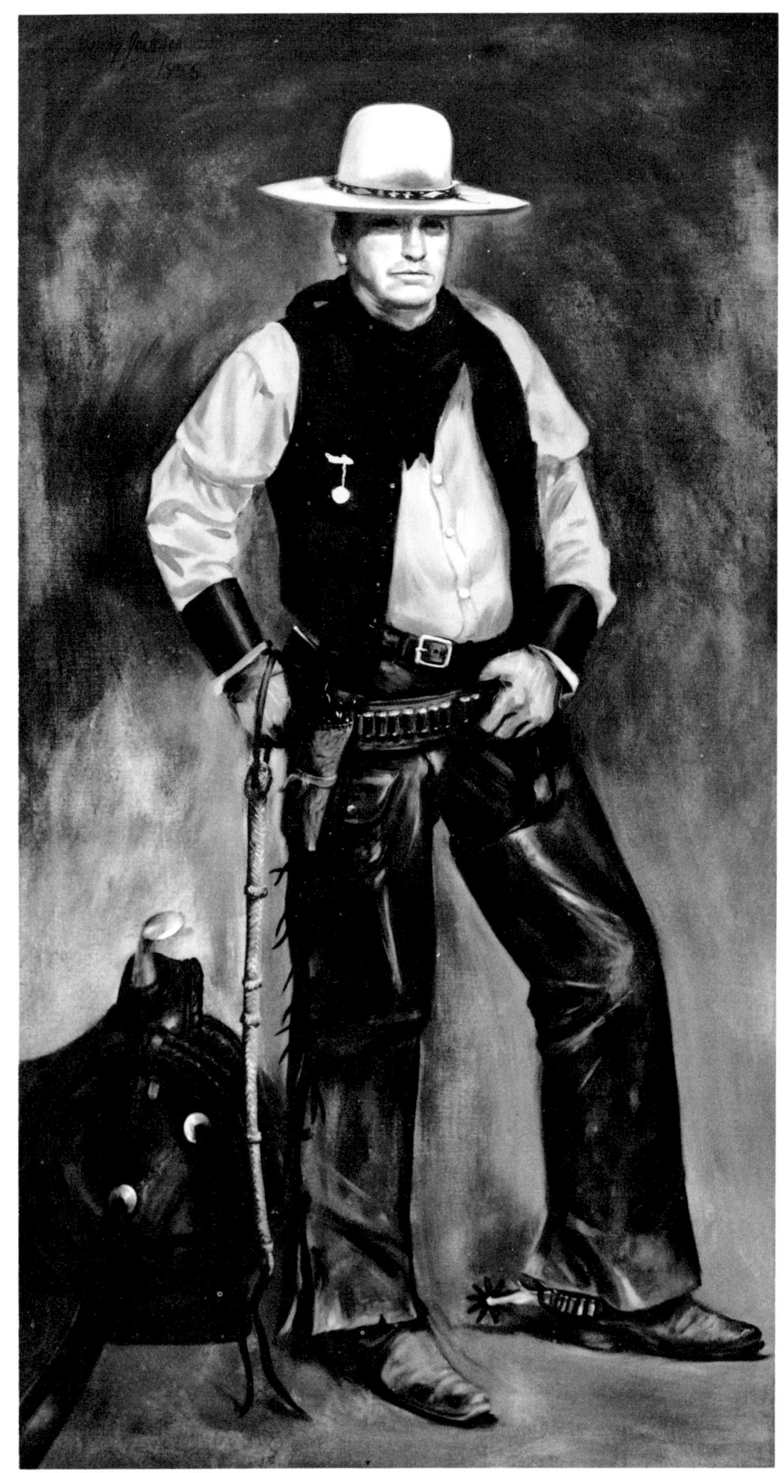

The Trail Driver, oil on canvas,
84¼ x 44", 1956
Buffalo Bill Historical Center

21

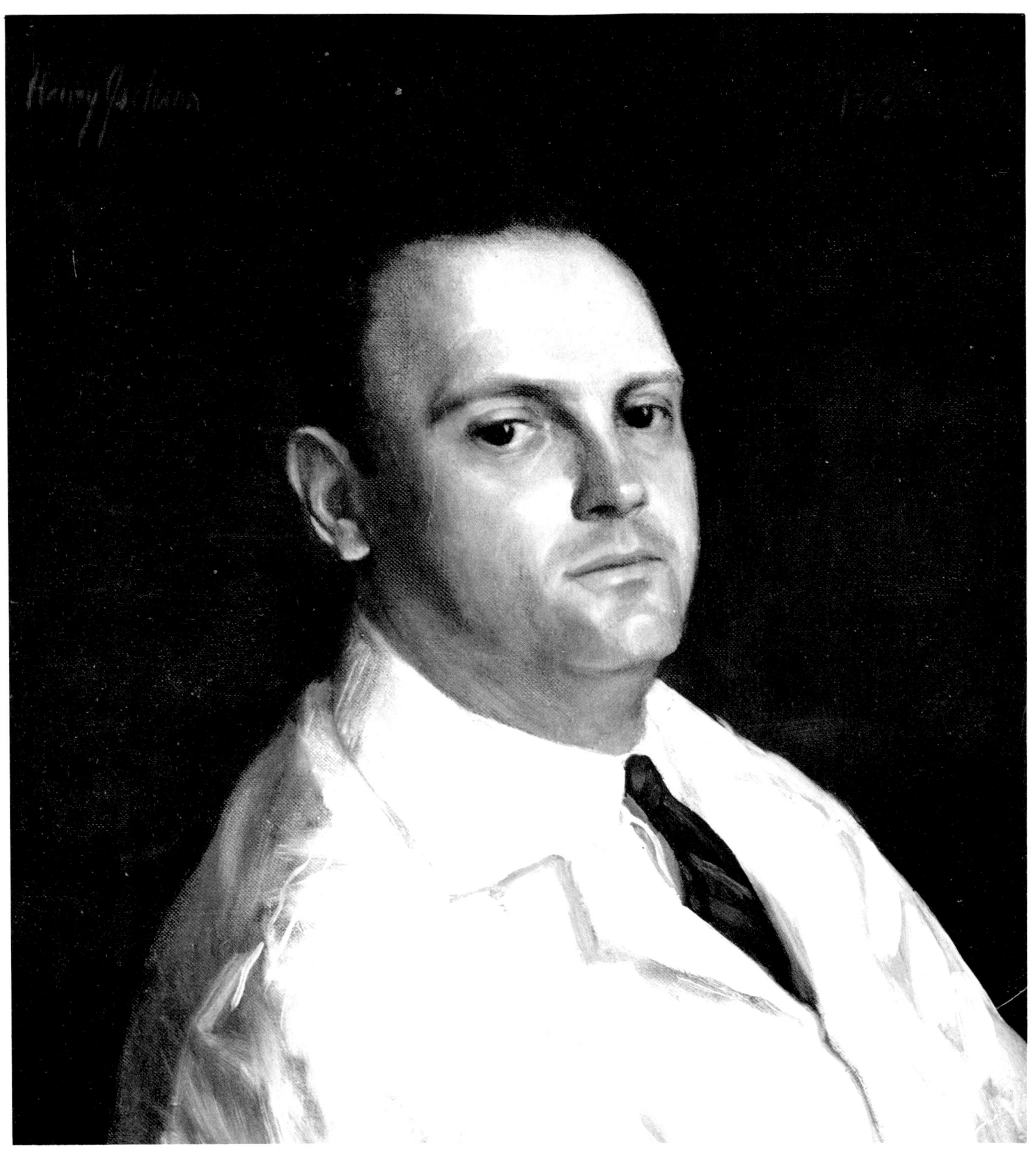

Portrait of a Physician,
oil on canvas,
23¾ x 21¾", 1962
Dr. Adrian W. Zorgniotti

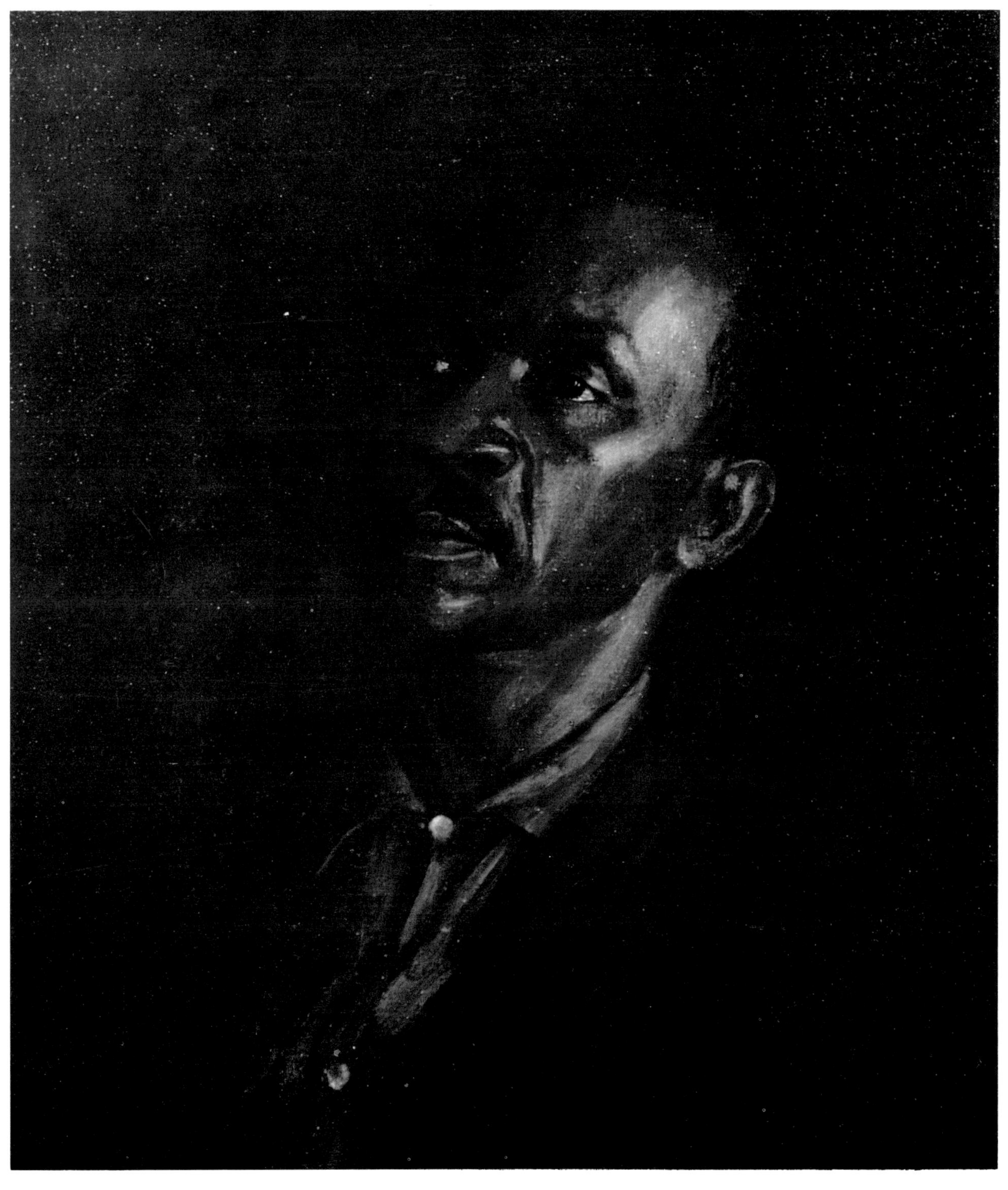

Frank Lamb, oil on canvas,
19¼ x 23″, 1963
Mrs. Adrian W. Zorgniotti

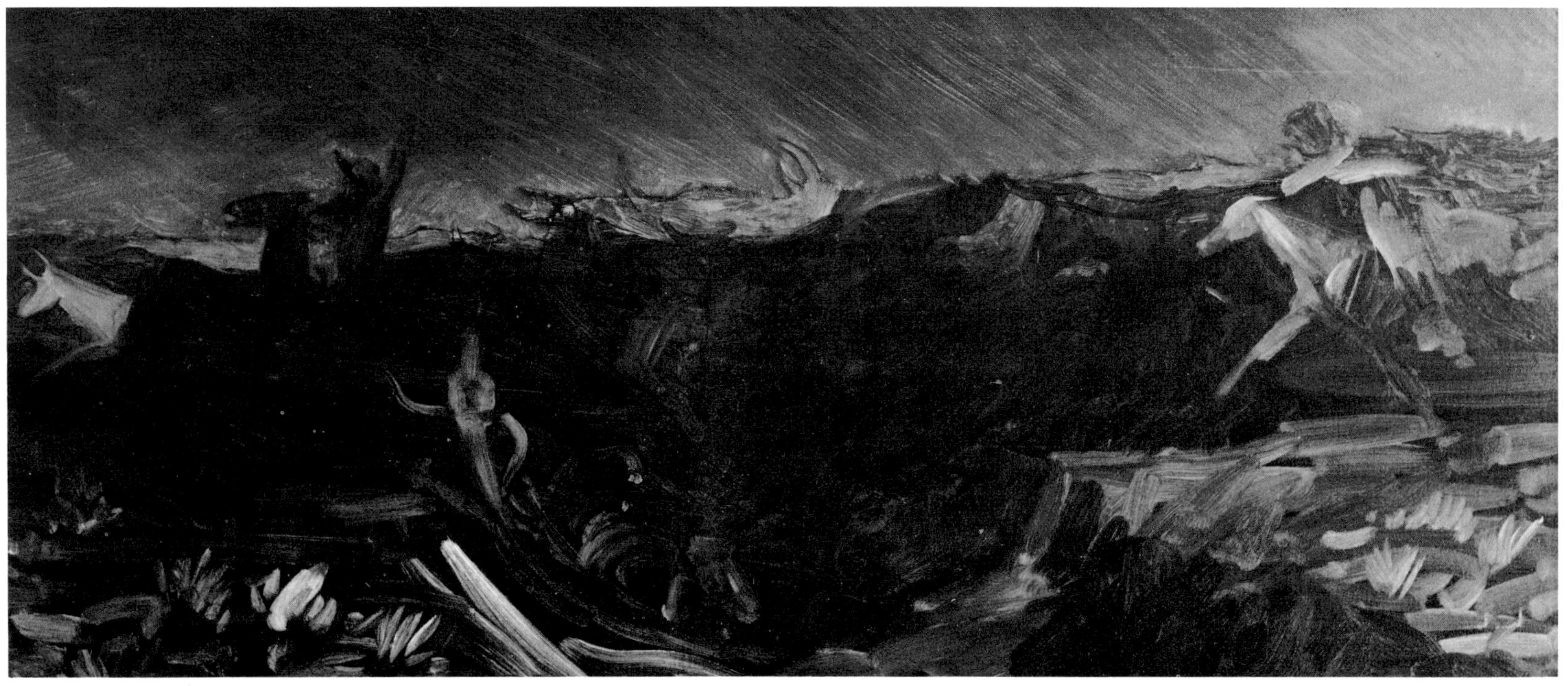

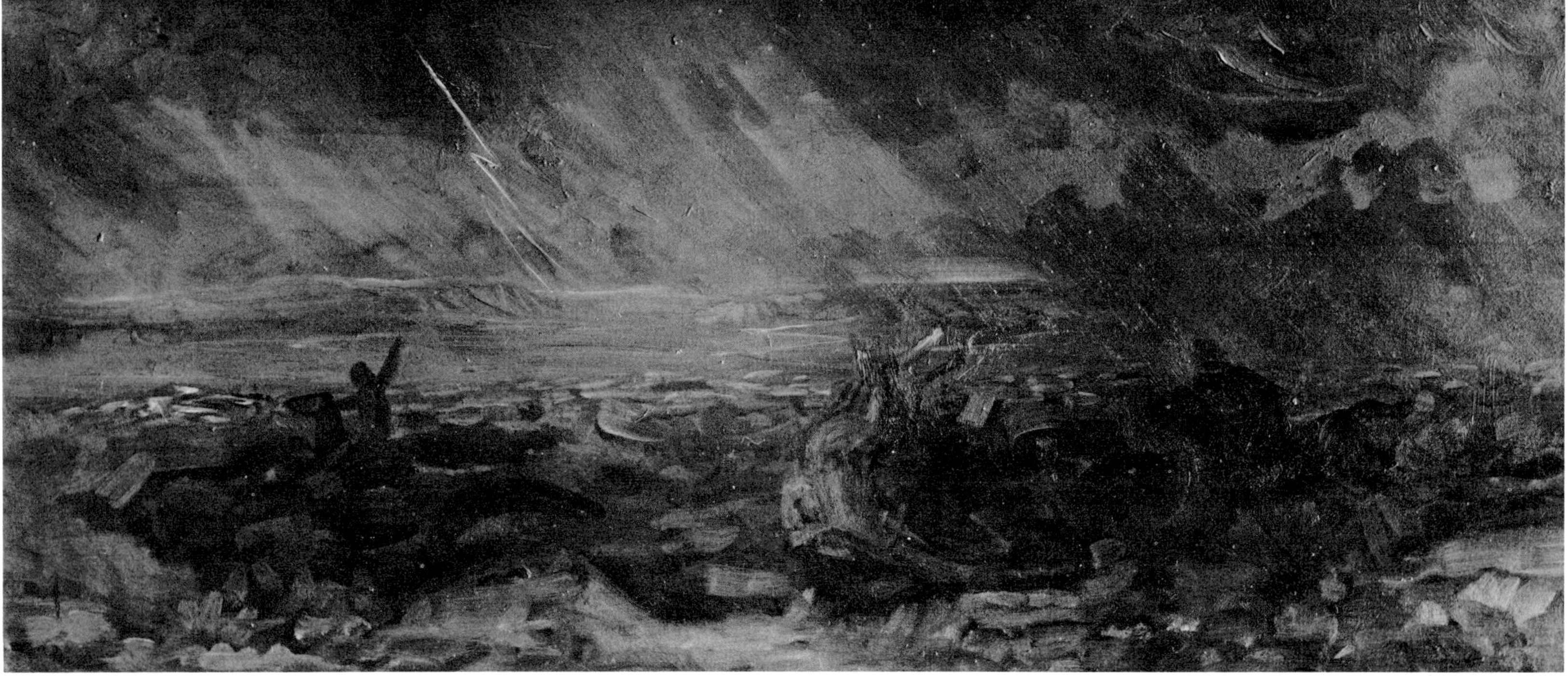

Four Studies for Stampede,
oil on canvas, 19 x 42", 1964
Wyoming Foundry Studios

His career represents a conscious
and sustained effort to transform
the substance of Western life into
the language of art.

Peter H. Hassrick in
Harry Jackson, 1981

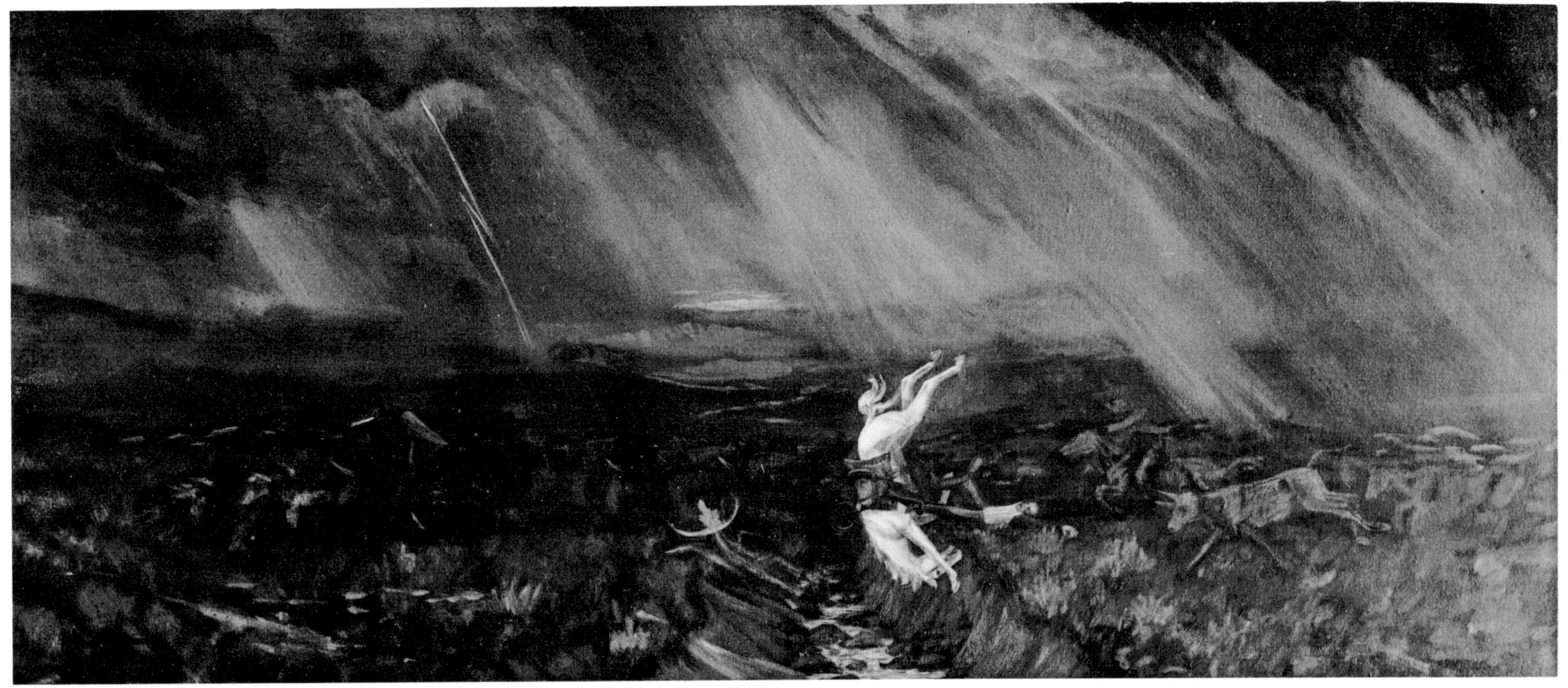

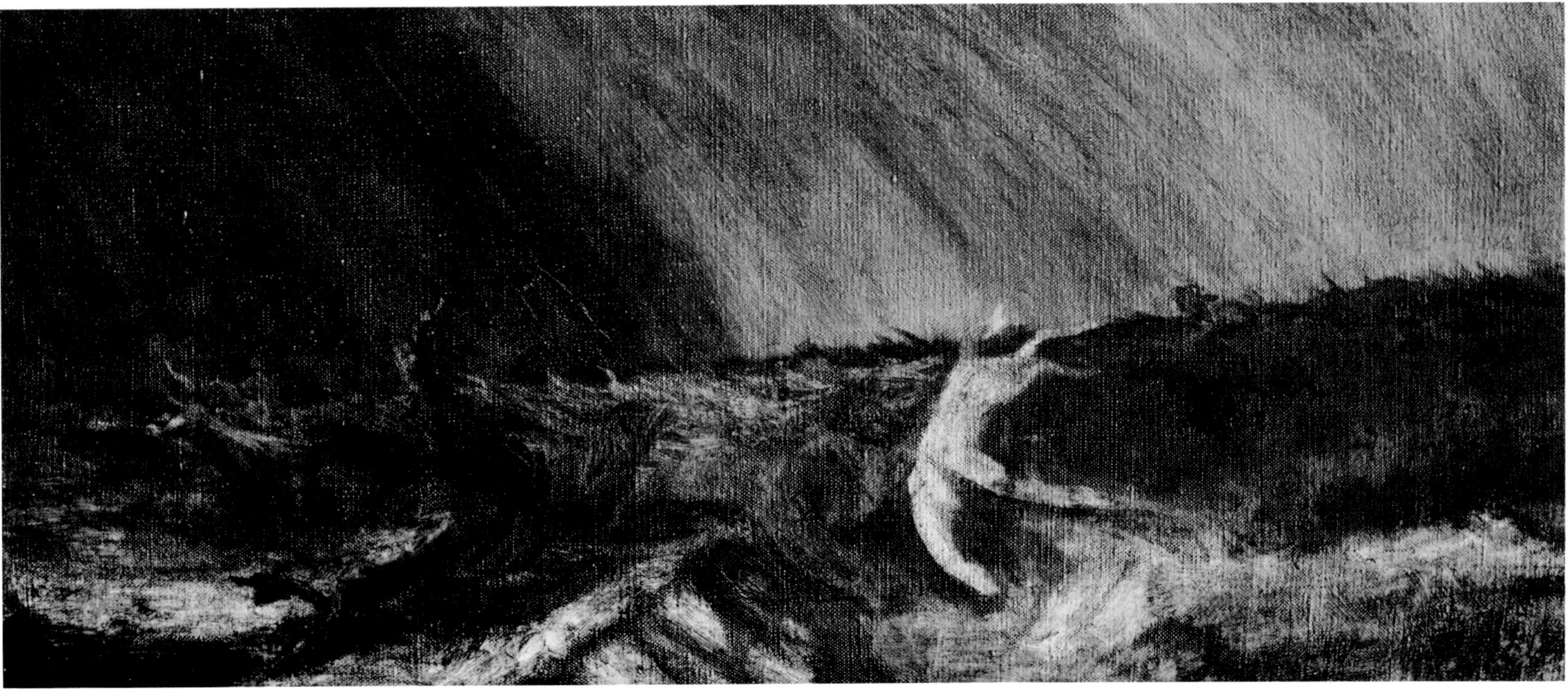

To find a painter with the ability to work in a representational style at a time when we were all surrounded by abstractionists and to find him capable of creating works of art as moving as these two immense canvases *(Stampede* and *Range Burial)* was a startling revelation.

Dr. John Walker in
Harry Jackson, 1981

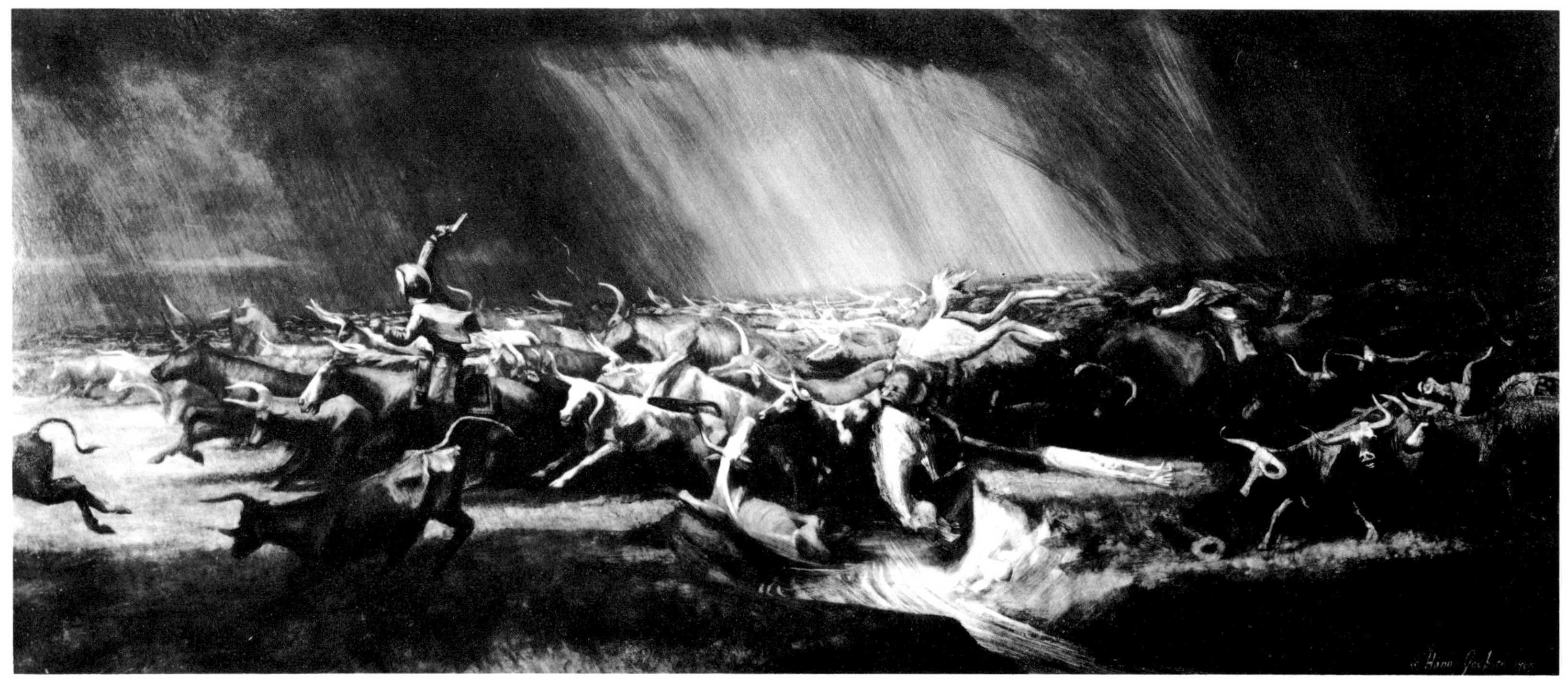

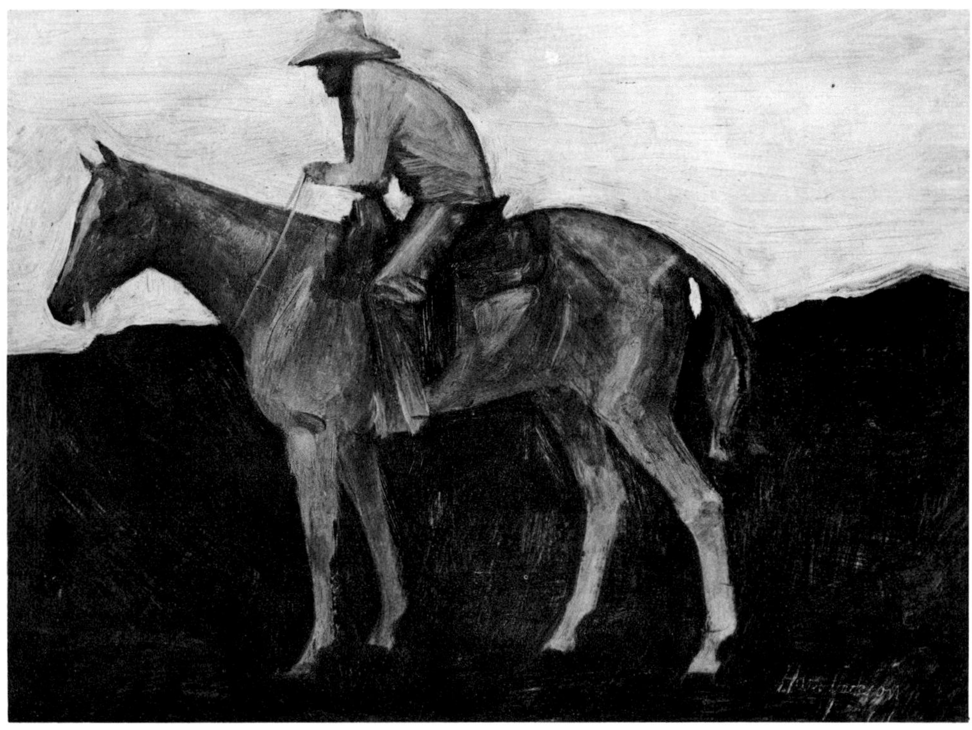

Final Study for Stampede,
egg tempera and oil on canvas,
22 x 48″, 1965
Wyoming Foundry Studios

Looking Things Over, oil on panel,
12 x 16″, 1964
Wyoming Foundry Studios

There are no "cowboys and
Indians" fake movie-melodrama in
these works, but factual subjects
treated with straight realism
dealing with something that every
cowpoke knows about.

Mario Amaya
The Connoisseur, 1979

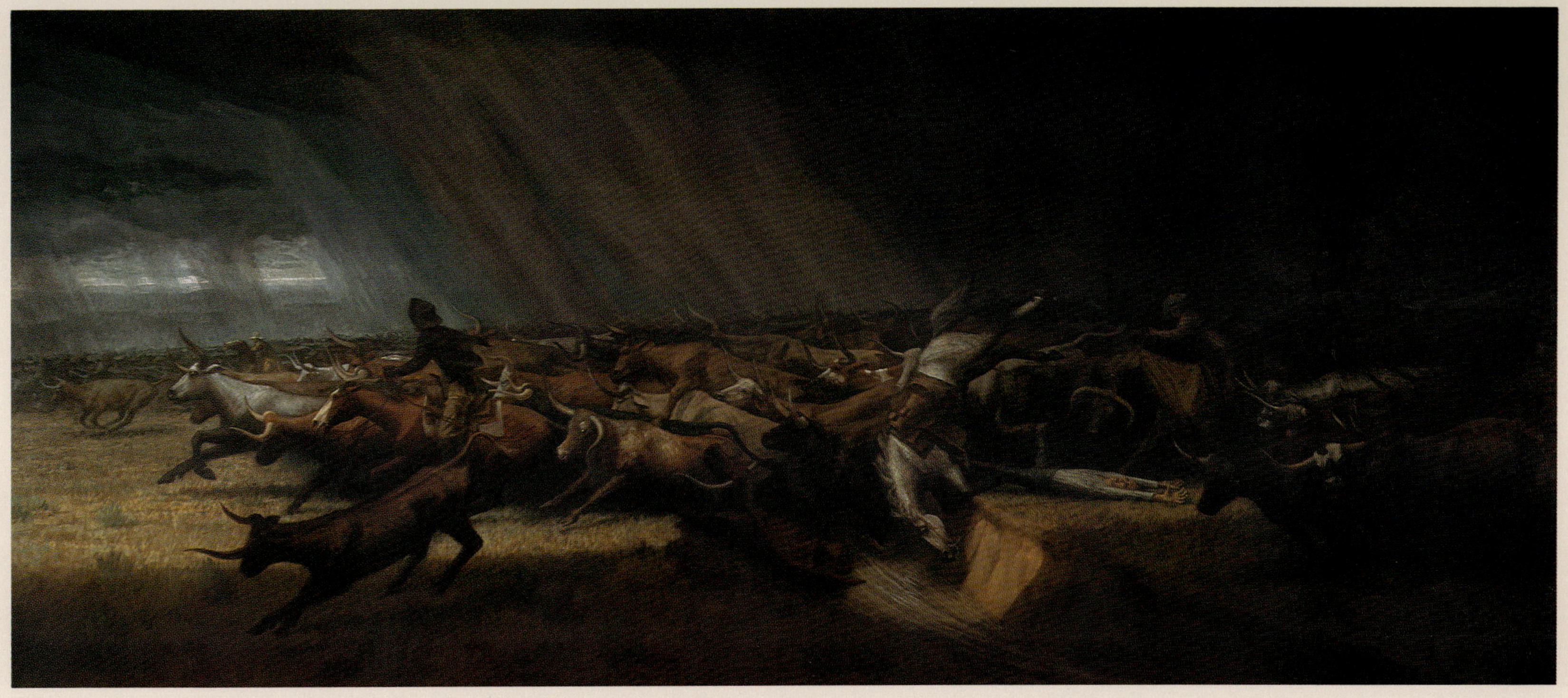

Stampede, oil on canvas,
10 x 21′, 1965
Buffalo Bill Historical Center

To know how completely he communicates as an artist you have only to consider the wide range of emotions expressed in his work: from the wild tumult of *Stampede* with the palpable terror of this animal cataclysm to the deeply affecting pathos of the heroic *Range Burial.*

Peter Hurd, 1965

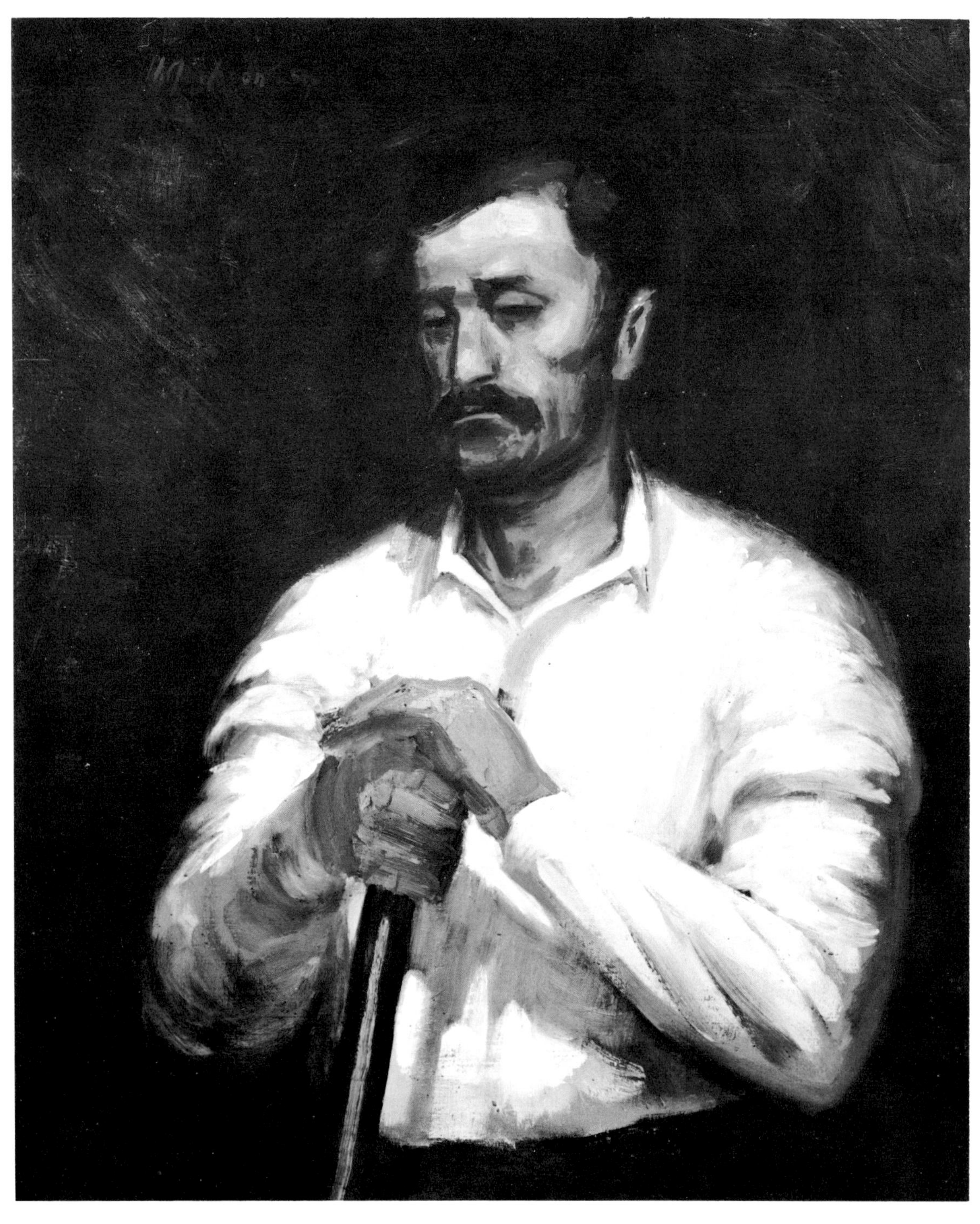

Portrait Study for Range Burial,
oil on canvas,
38¾ x 30⅞", 1959
Mrs. Henry H.R. Coe

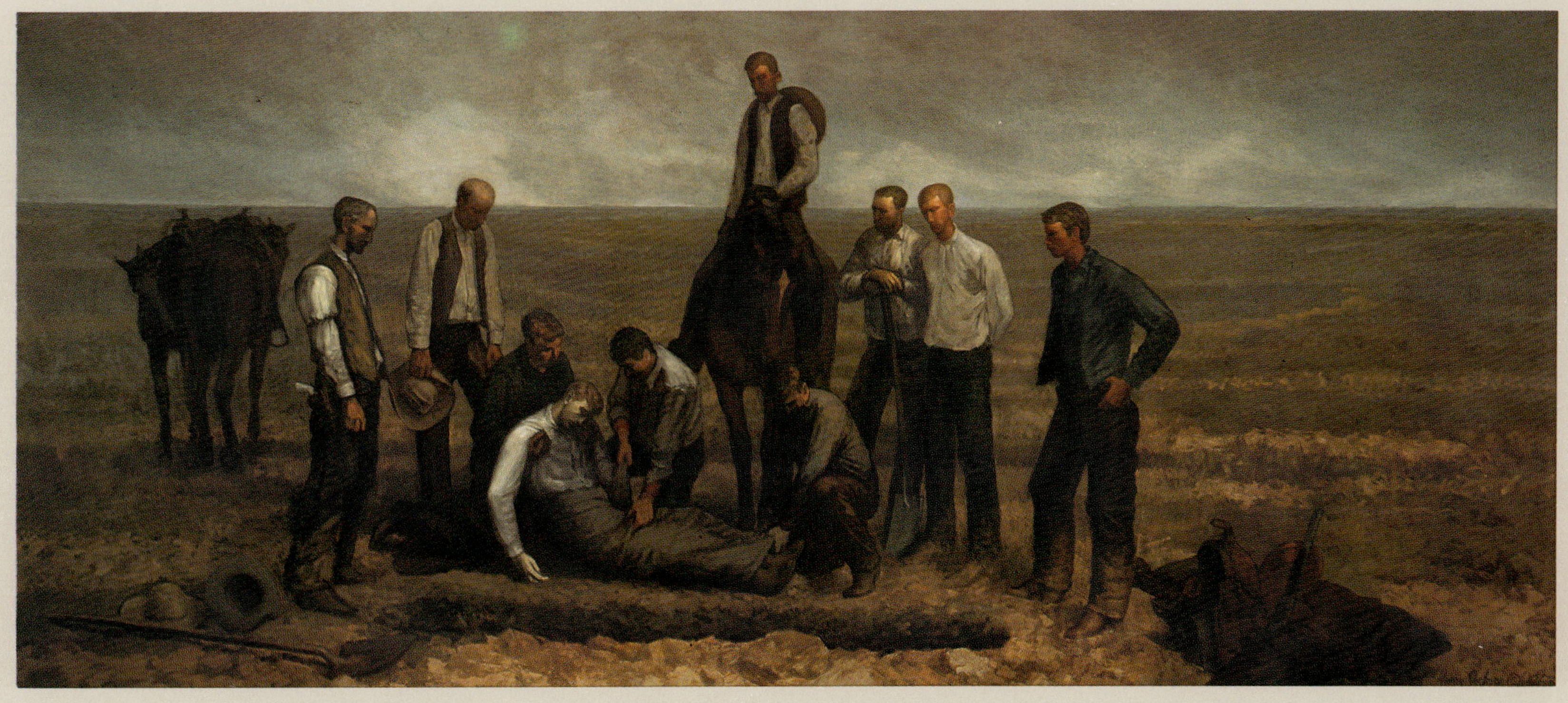

Range Burial, oil on canvas,
10 x 21', 1963
Buffalo Bill Historical Center

No holds are barred in
contemporary painting and a
strong grip taken on traditional
narrative styles in Harry Jackson's
mammoth elegaic canvas, *The
Range Burial* . . .

Stuart Preston
New York Times, 1964

The Bronzes

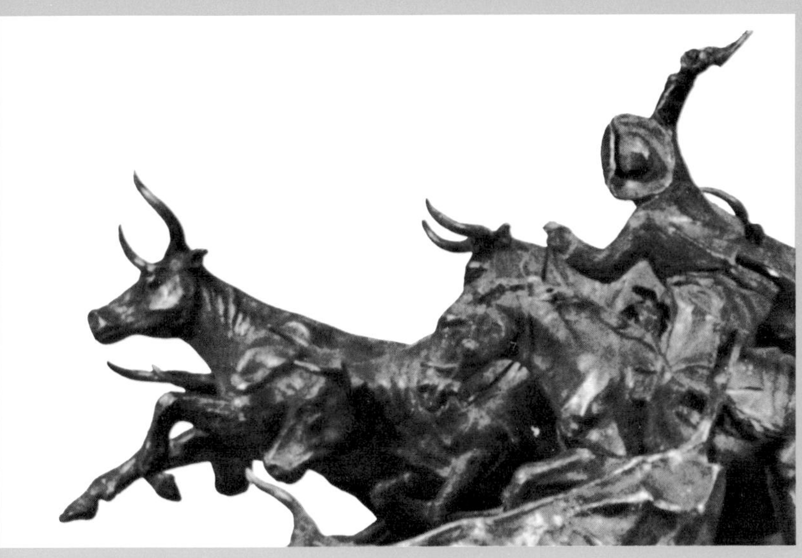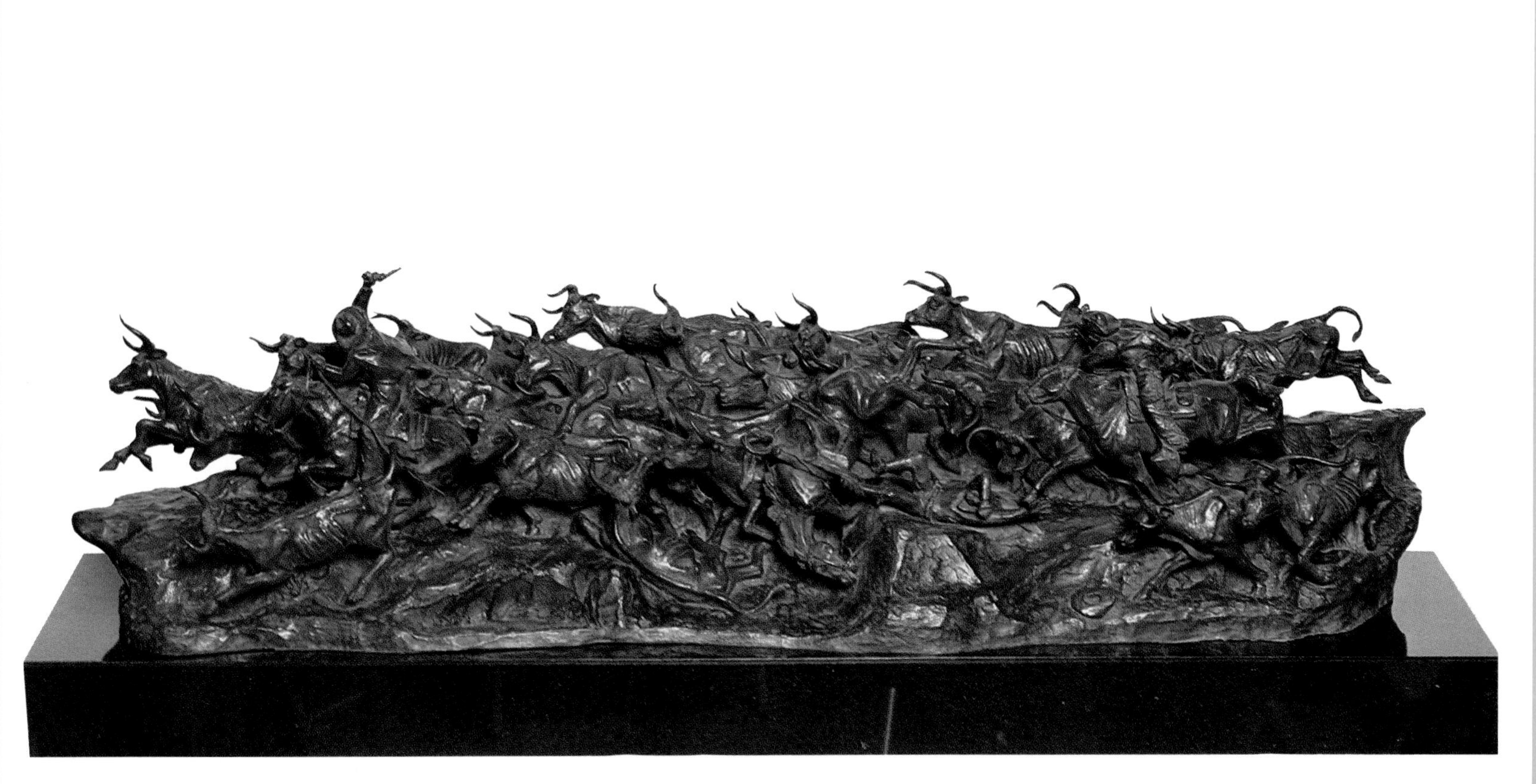

Stampede, bronze,
53⅜ x 14¼ x 14¼ ", 1959
Buffalo Bill Historical Center

His cowboys battle a thundering stampede, sing their long ballads, rope their steers and, in solemn ritual bury a friend under the big sky. They manage to combine power and tenderness.

Time Magazine, 1960

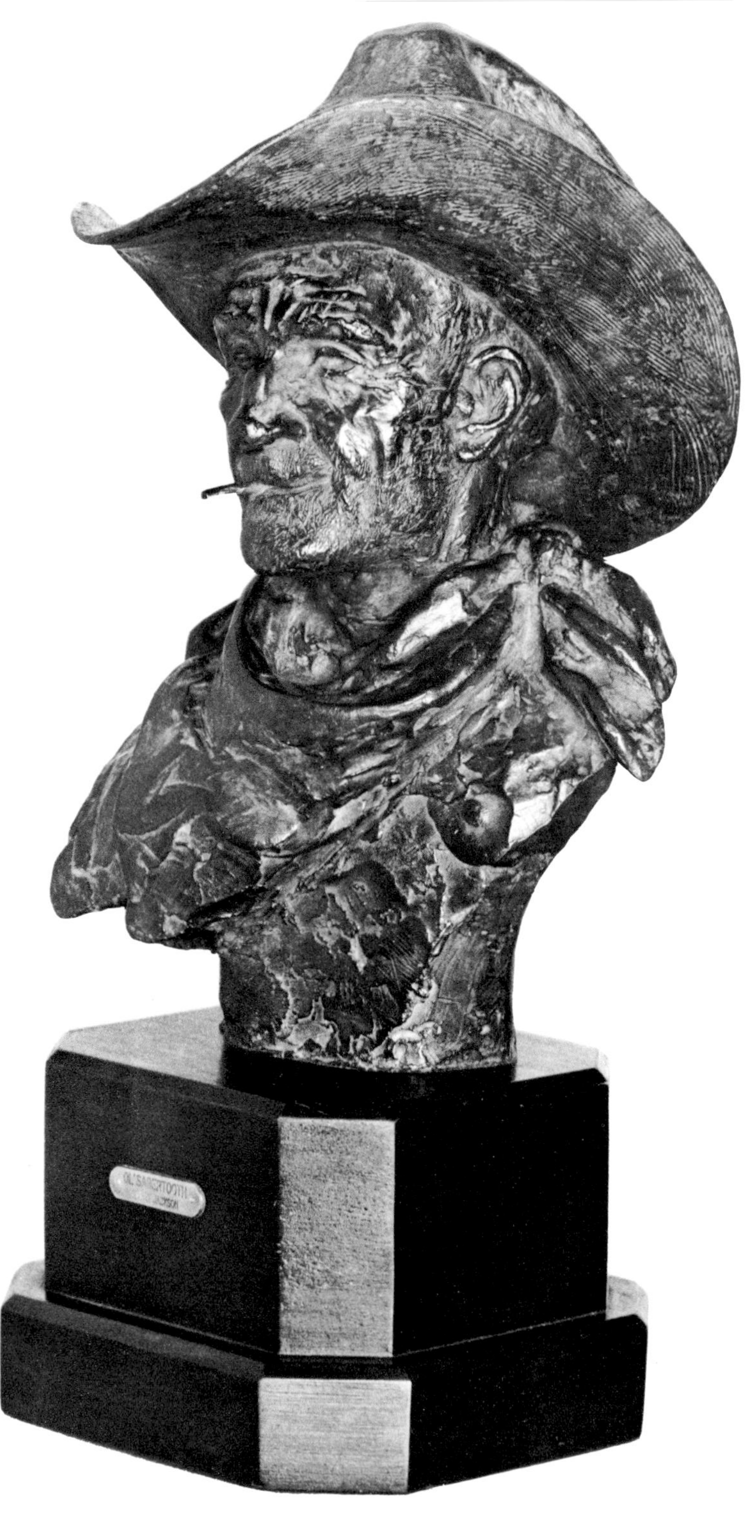

Ol Sabertooth, bronze,
10 x 6½ x 6¼ ", 1980
Wyoming Foundry Studios

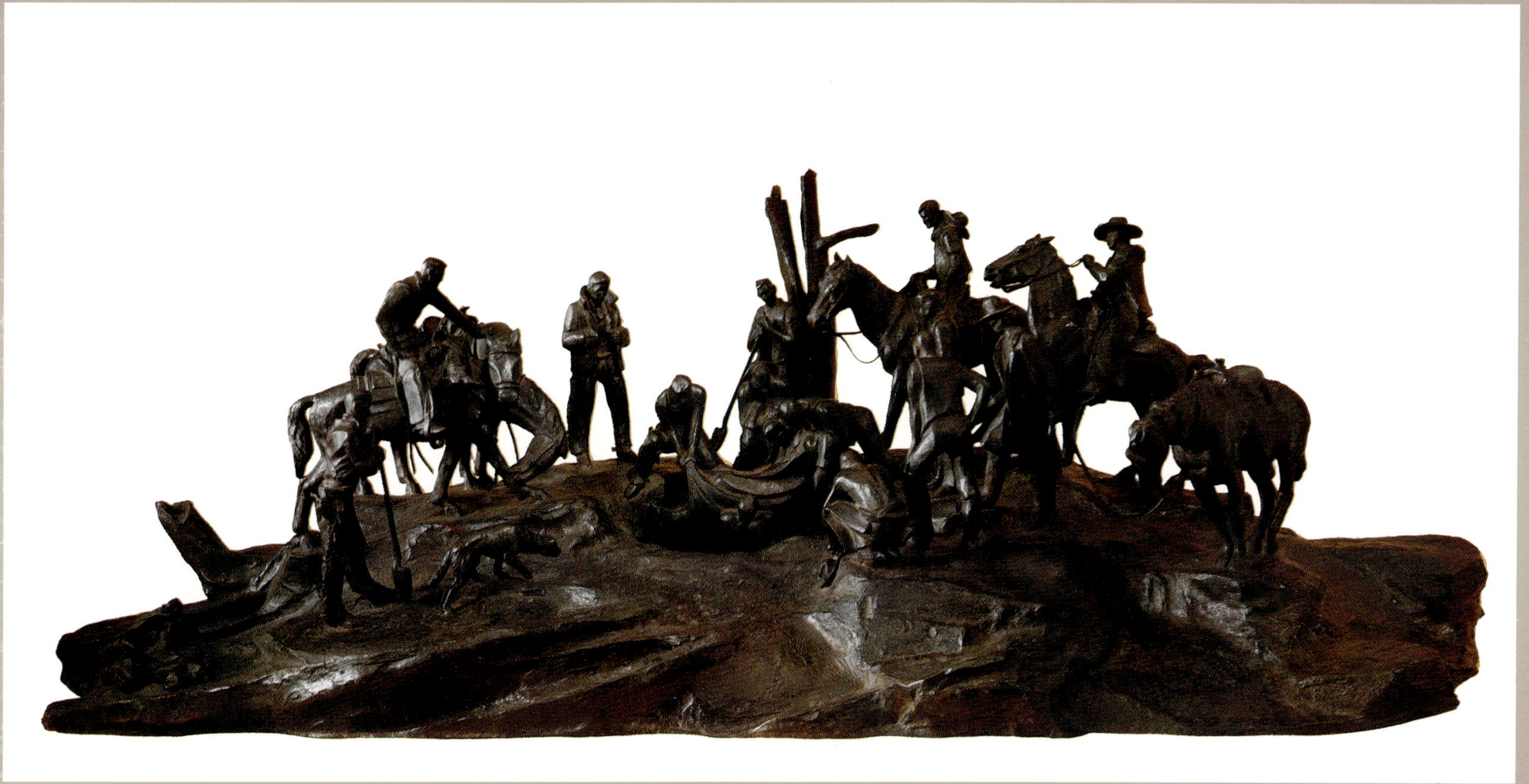

Range Burial, bronze,
15 x 43 x 23", 1958
Buffalo Bill Historical Center

The group around the open grave is a figure composition rarely seen in bronze in our time, free standing, with air among them, fully realized as individual pieces and as a group.

Frank Getlein
Washington Star, 1964

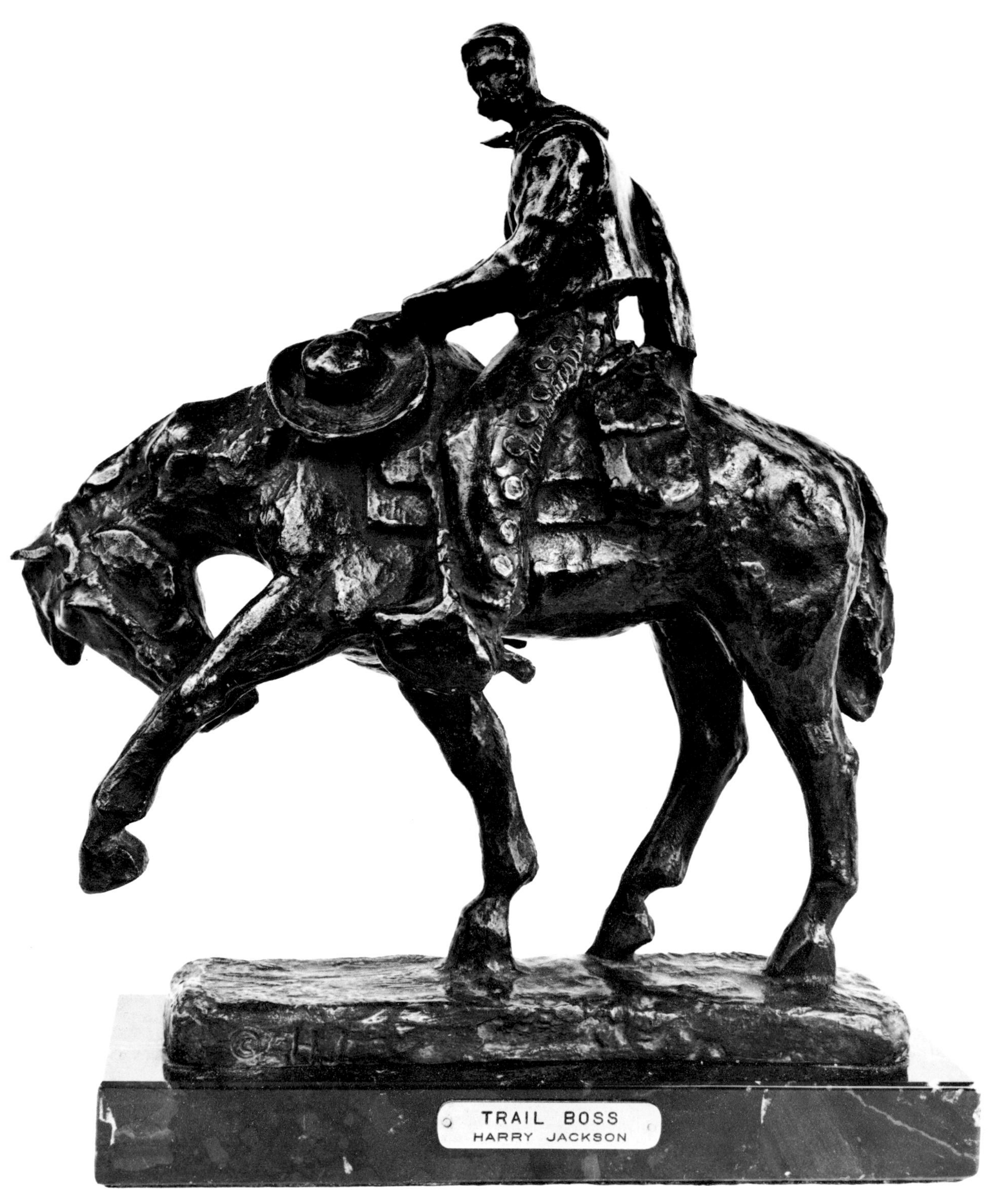

Trail Boss, bronze,
8¼ x 8 x 3¼", 1958
Wyoming Foundry Studios

34

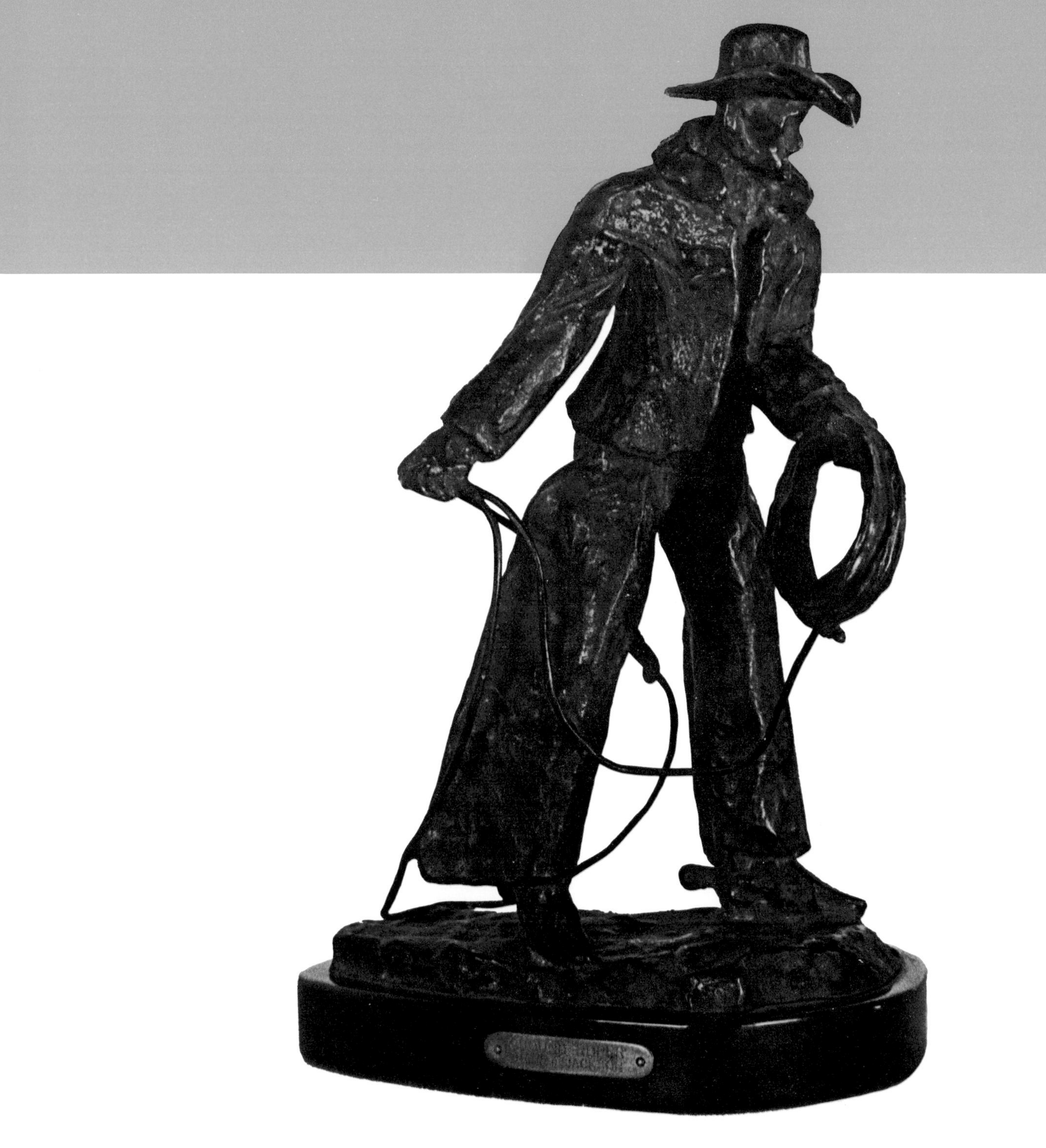

Ground Roper, bronze,
10 x 5 x 4", 1958
Wyoming Foundry Studios

Of them all, Harry Jackson has
made this place his own. America's
most famous sculptor of Wild West
subjects in our time, the man whose
very name conjures up "Cowboy," . . .

Mario Amaya
The Connoisseur, 1979

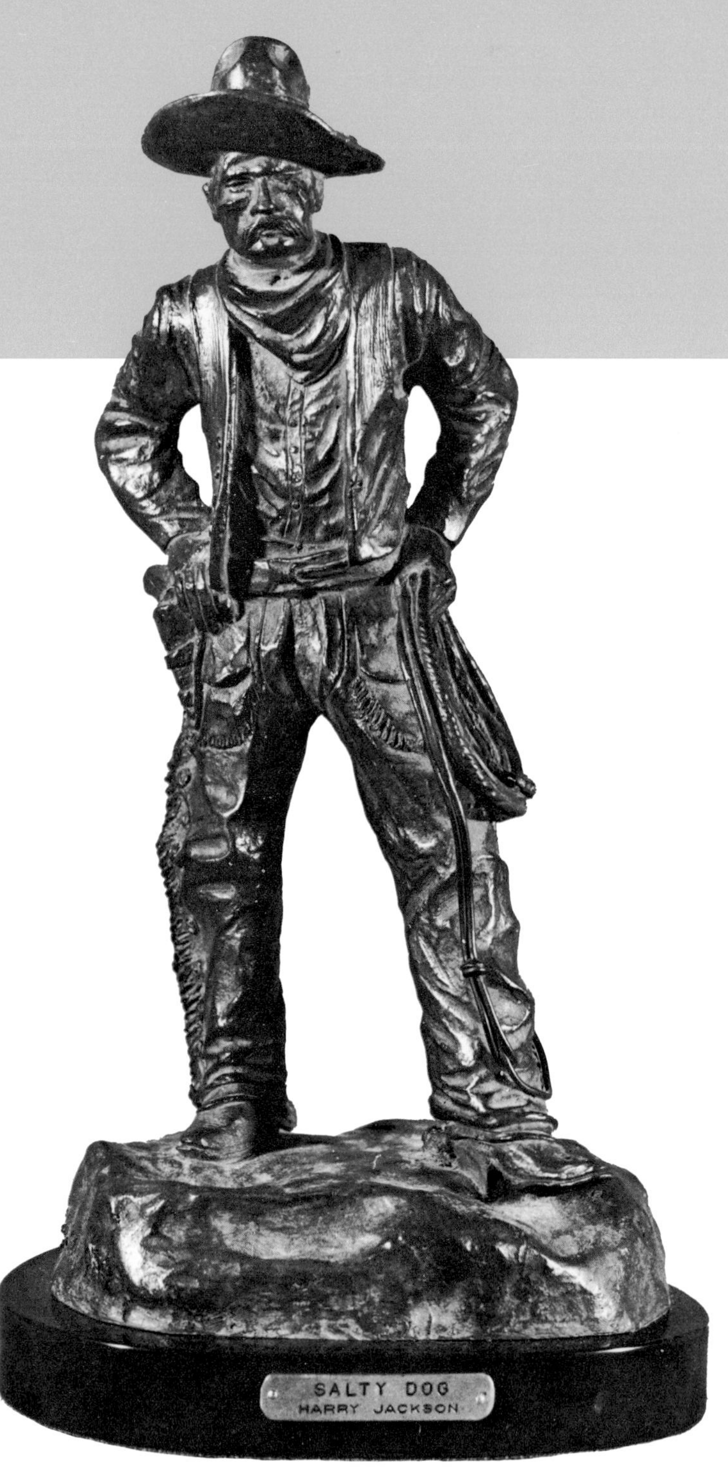

Salty Dog, bronze,
10¼ x 5 x 4½", 1959
Wyoming Foundry Studios

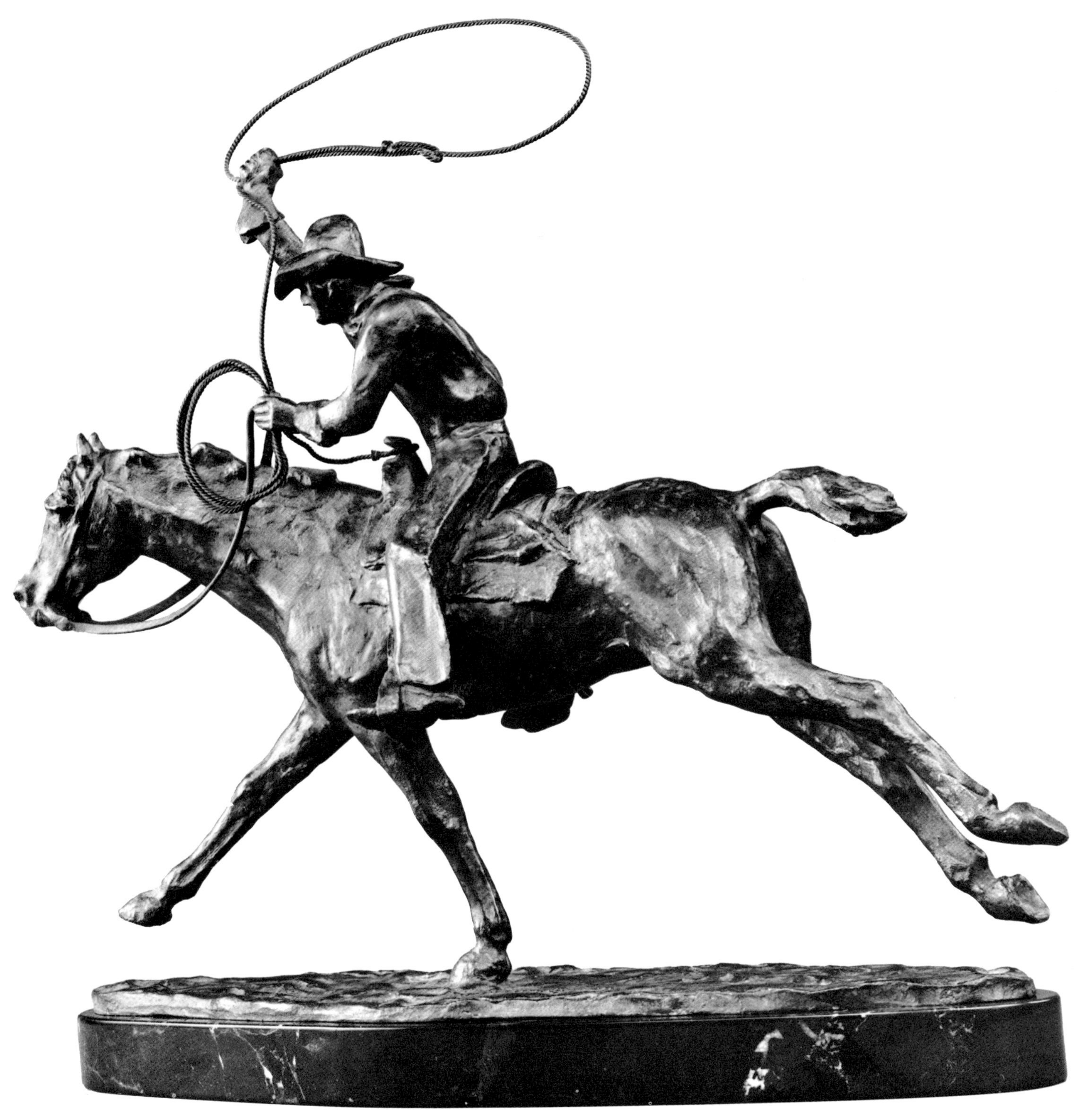

Ropin', bronze,
13½ x 17½ x 5¼ ", 1959
Wyoming Foundry Studios

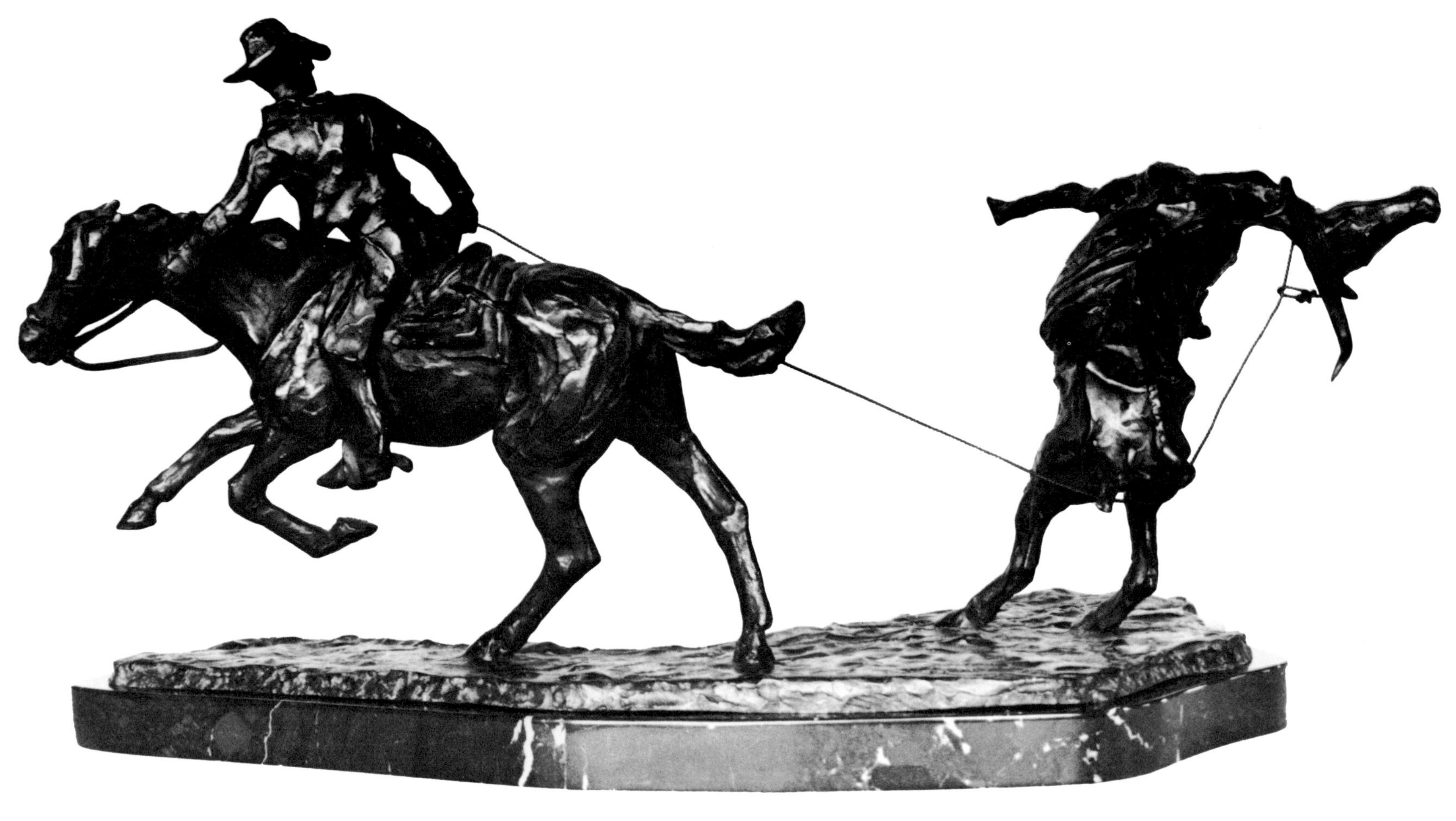

Steer Roper, Hard and Fast,
bronze, 12 x 25 x 12″, 1959
Buffalo Bill Historical Center

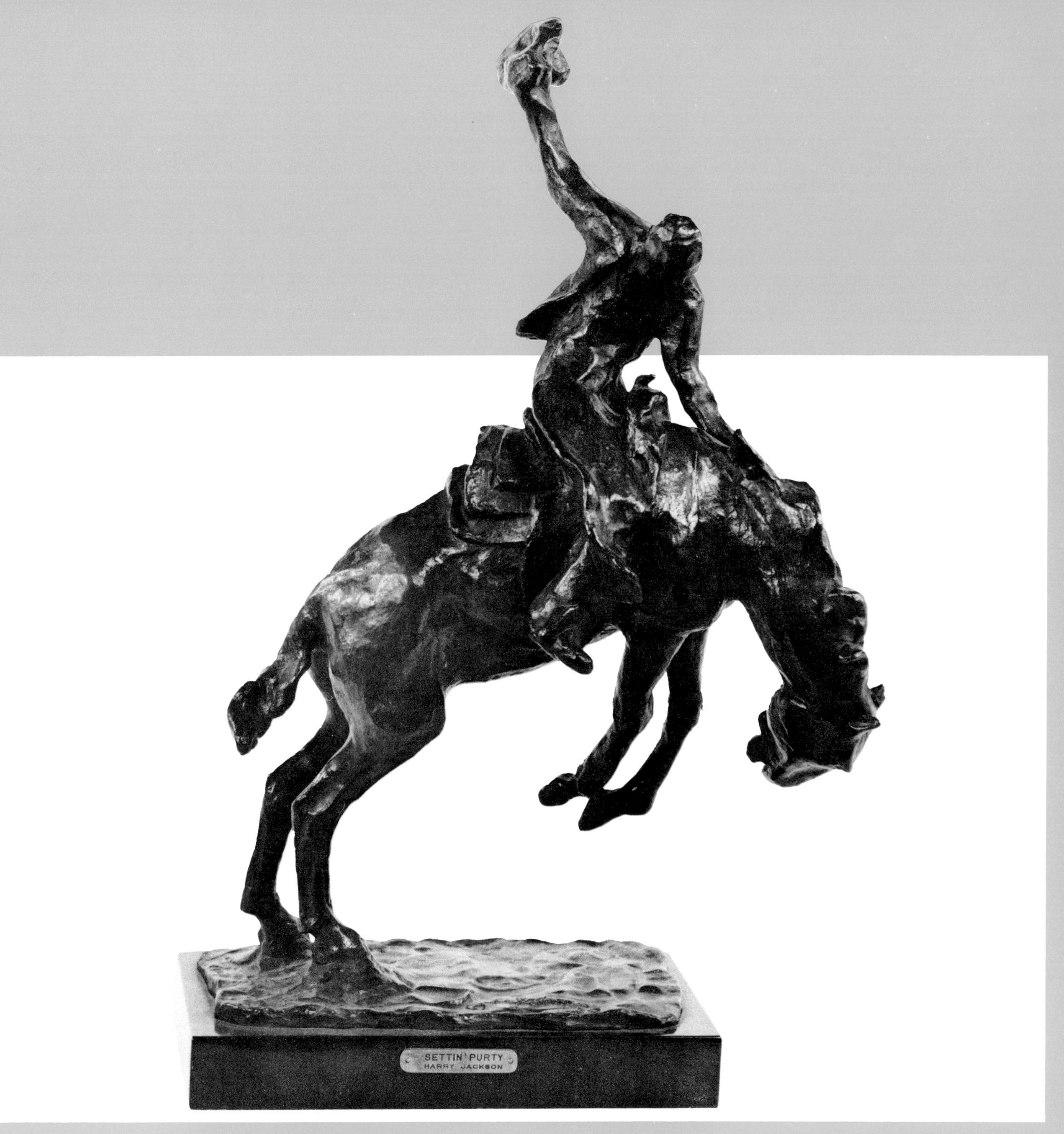

Settin' Purty, bronze,
16 x 10¼ x 6″, 1959
Wyoming Foundry Studios

The pure force generated by
holding two straining masses
together with a single taut wire . . .
adds an indefinable sense of power
and hypnotic balance to this
excellently modeled bronze.

Frank Getlein
Harry Jackson, 1969

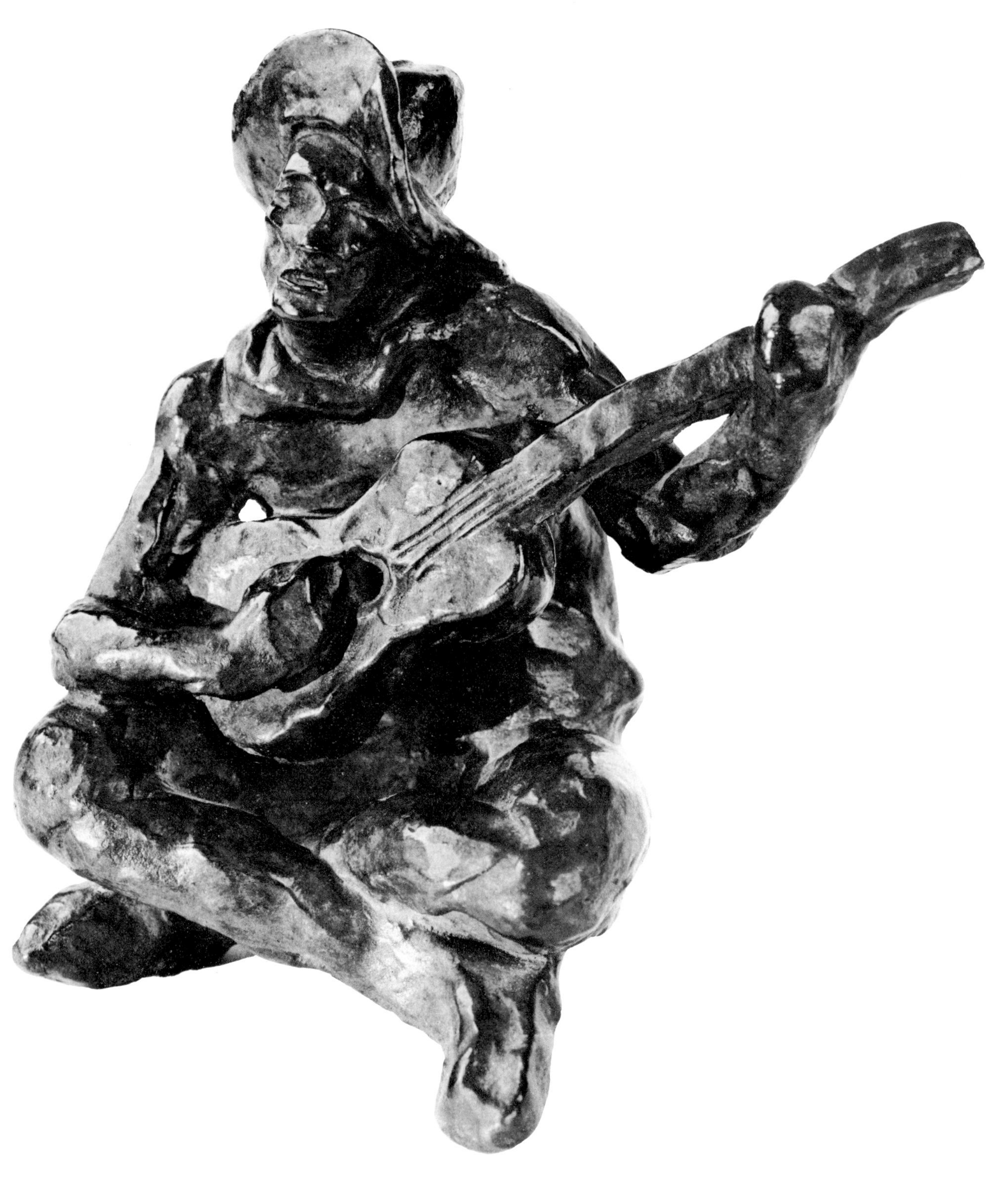

Long Ballad, bronze,
6 x 5 x 4″, 1959
Buffalo Bill Historical Center

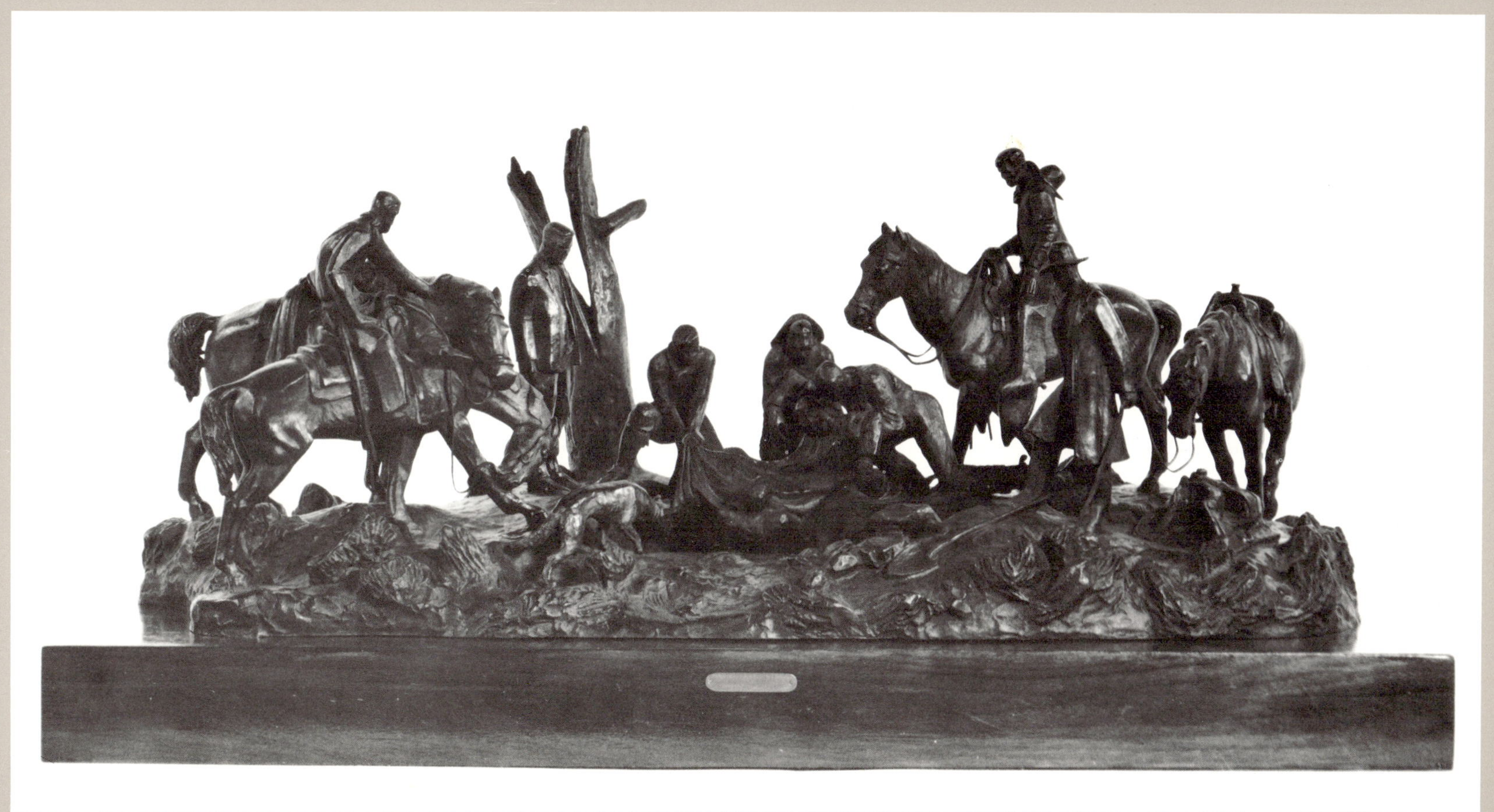

Plantin', bronze,
13 x 26½ x 12½ ", 1960
Wyoming Foundry Studios

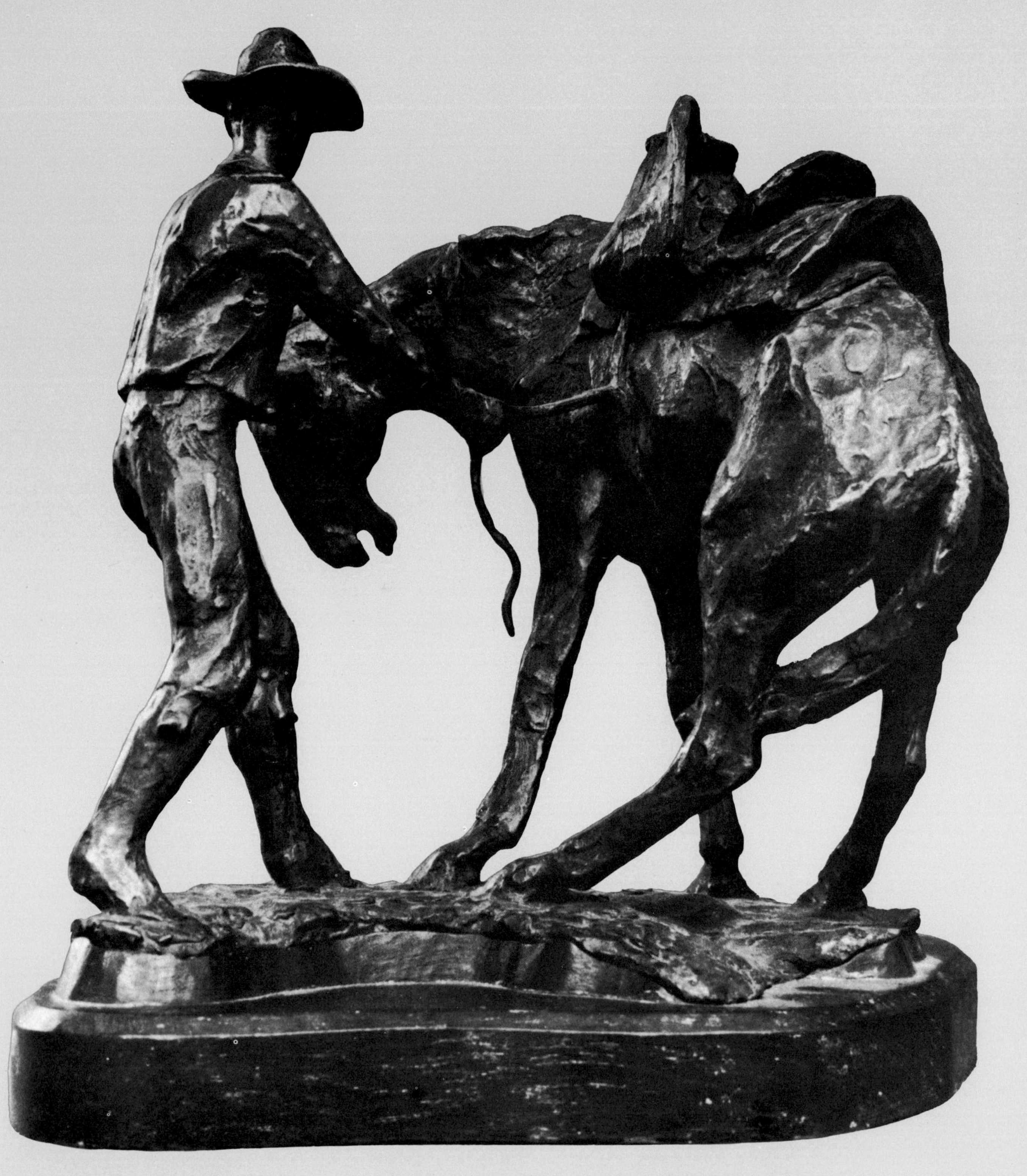

First Saddle, bronze,
12 x 11¼ x 3¾″, 1961
Wyoming Foundry Studios

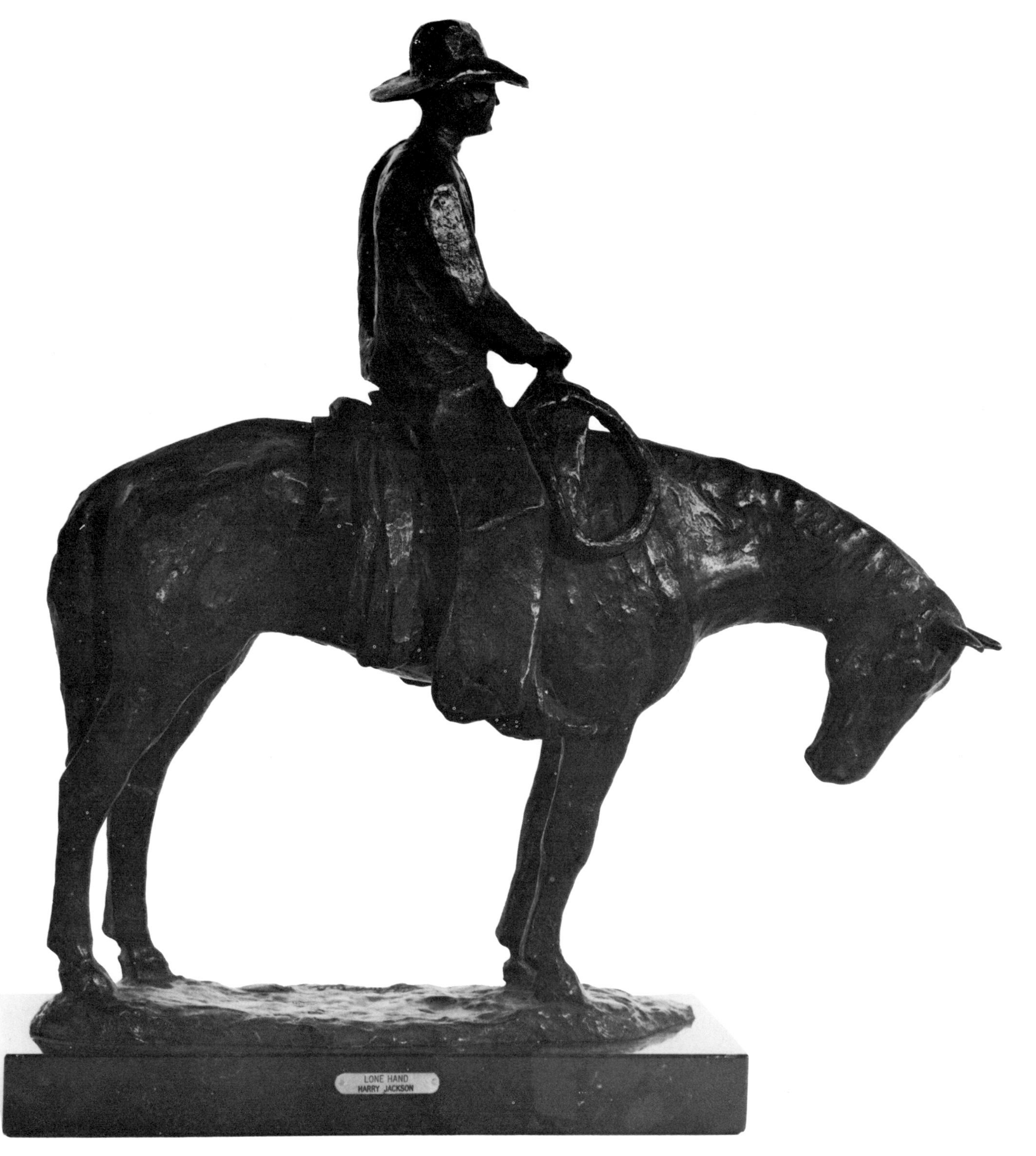

Lone Hand, bronze,
15 x 15 x 6", 1961
Buffalo Bill Historical Center

Everyday, nearly, I look at *The Lone Hand.* Nobody ever made a better back-sag than you've made. He is my people. The whole thing is life to me.

J. Frank Dobie, c. 1969

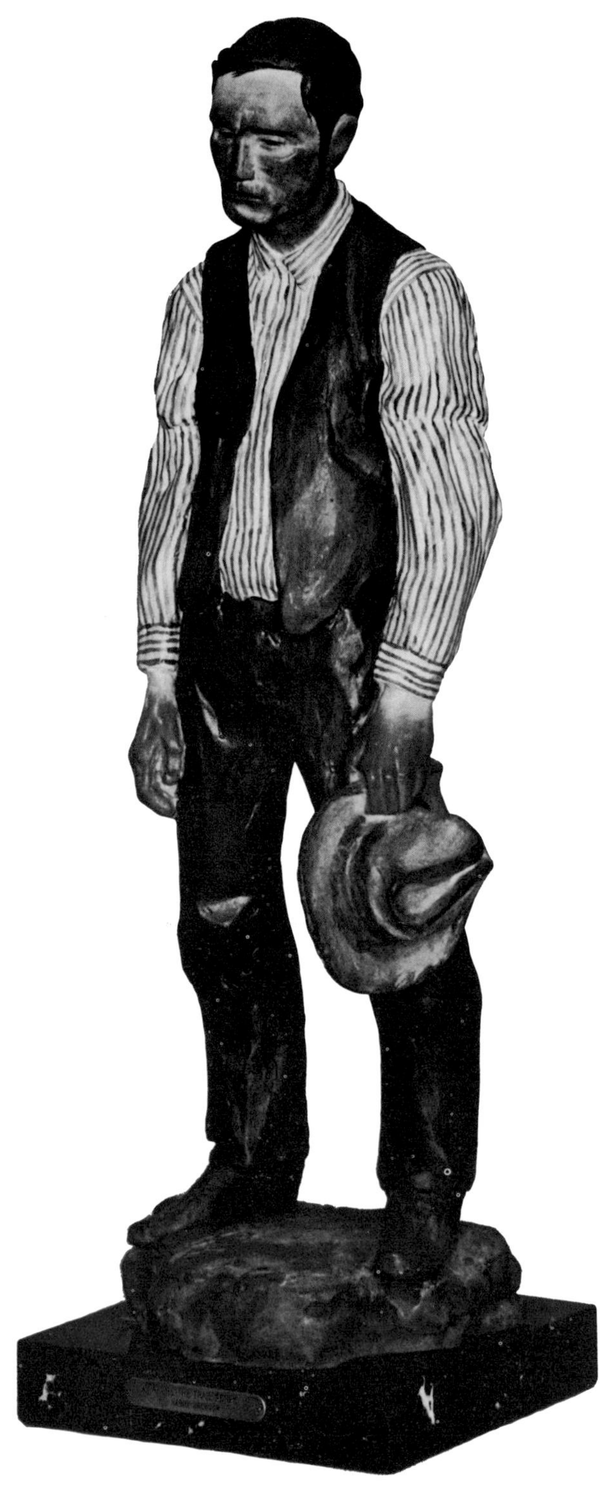

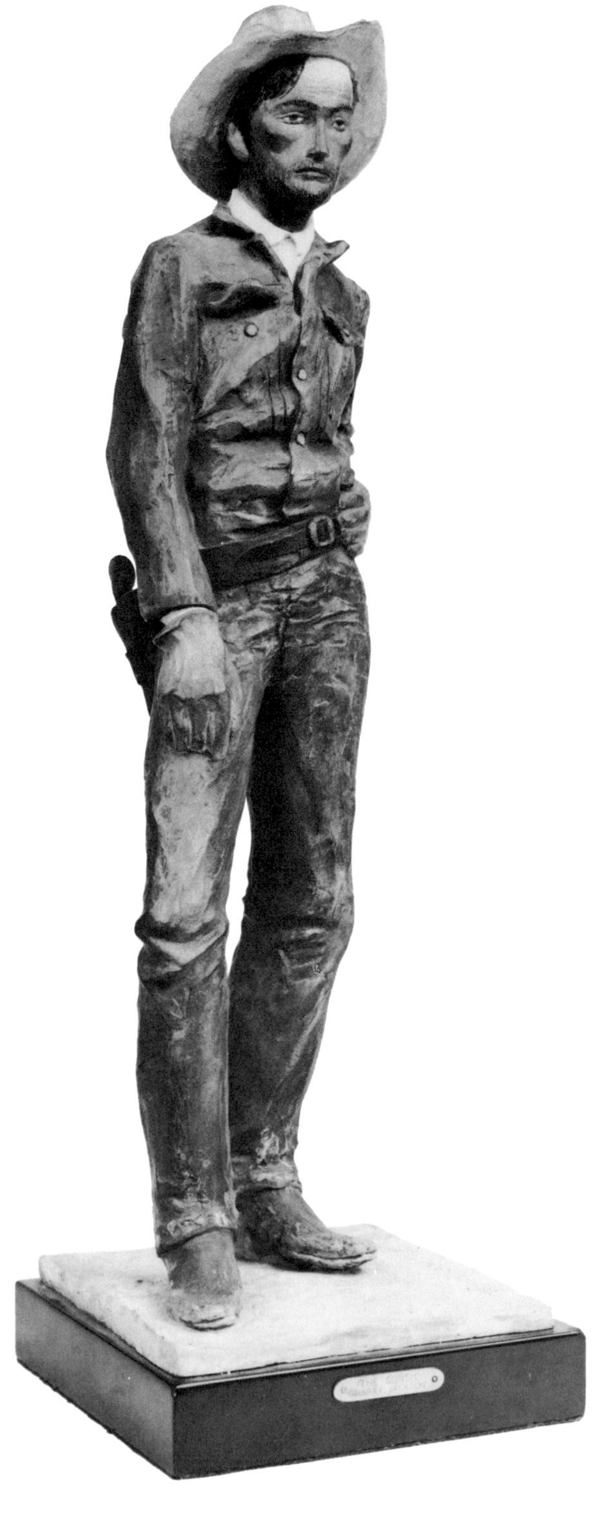

Where the Trail Forks,
polychrome bronze,
19½ x 5¾ x 5½", 1962
Wyoming Foundry Studios

. . . a cocky kid, a little too big for
his britches, given to throwing
about what weight he has and
enthralled with the idea of himself
as a man in a man's world.

Frank Getlein
Harry Jackson, 1969

Gunsil, polychrome bronze,
18⅛ x 6¼ x 6", 1962
Buffalo Bill Historical Center

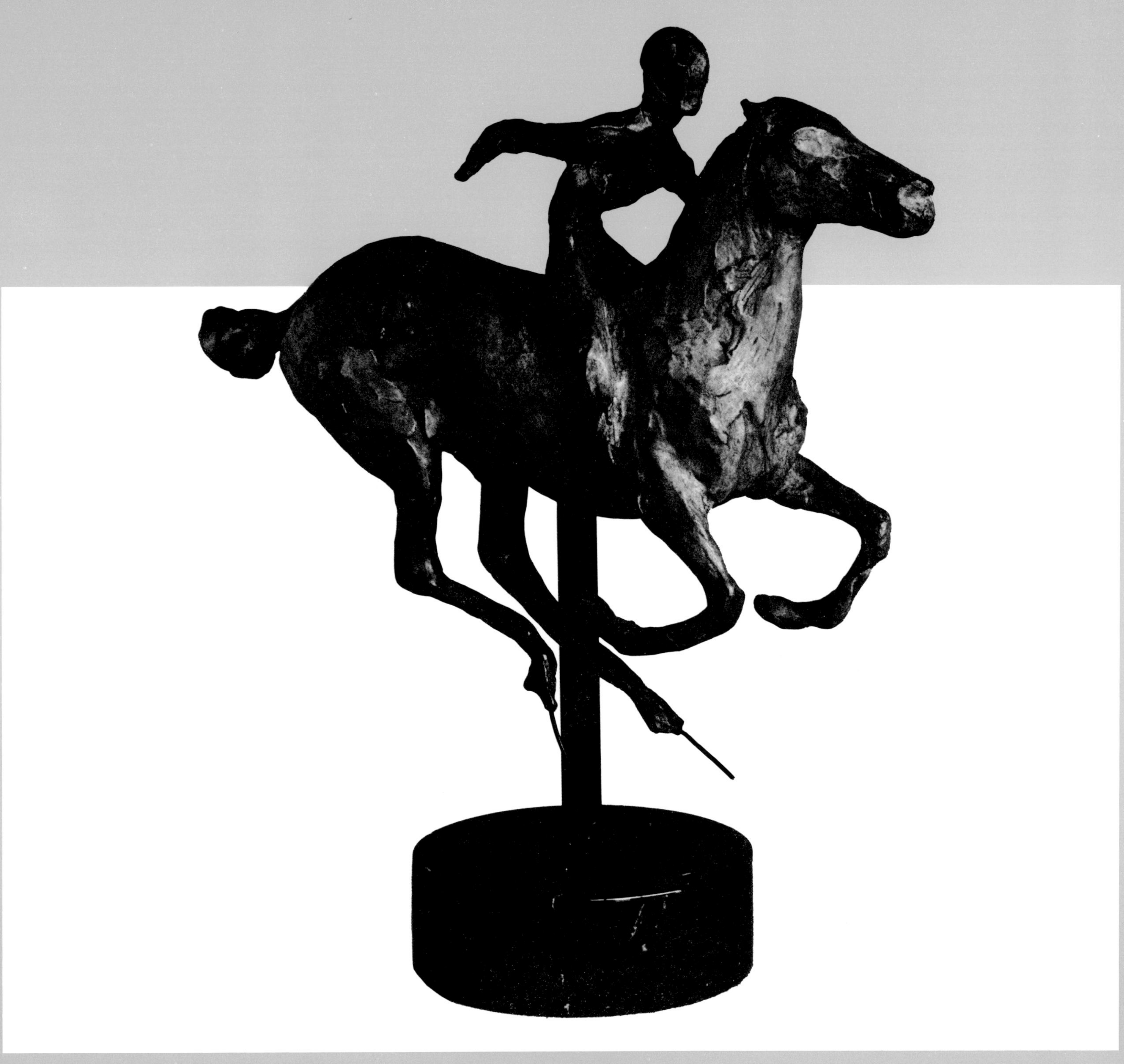

*Pony Express — Unfinished
Sketch*, bronze,
10¾ x 11½ x 2¾″, 1968
Wyoming Foundry Studios

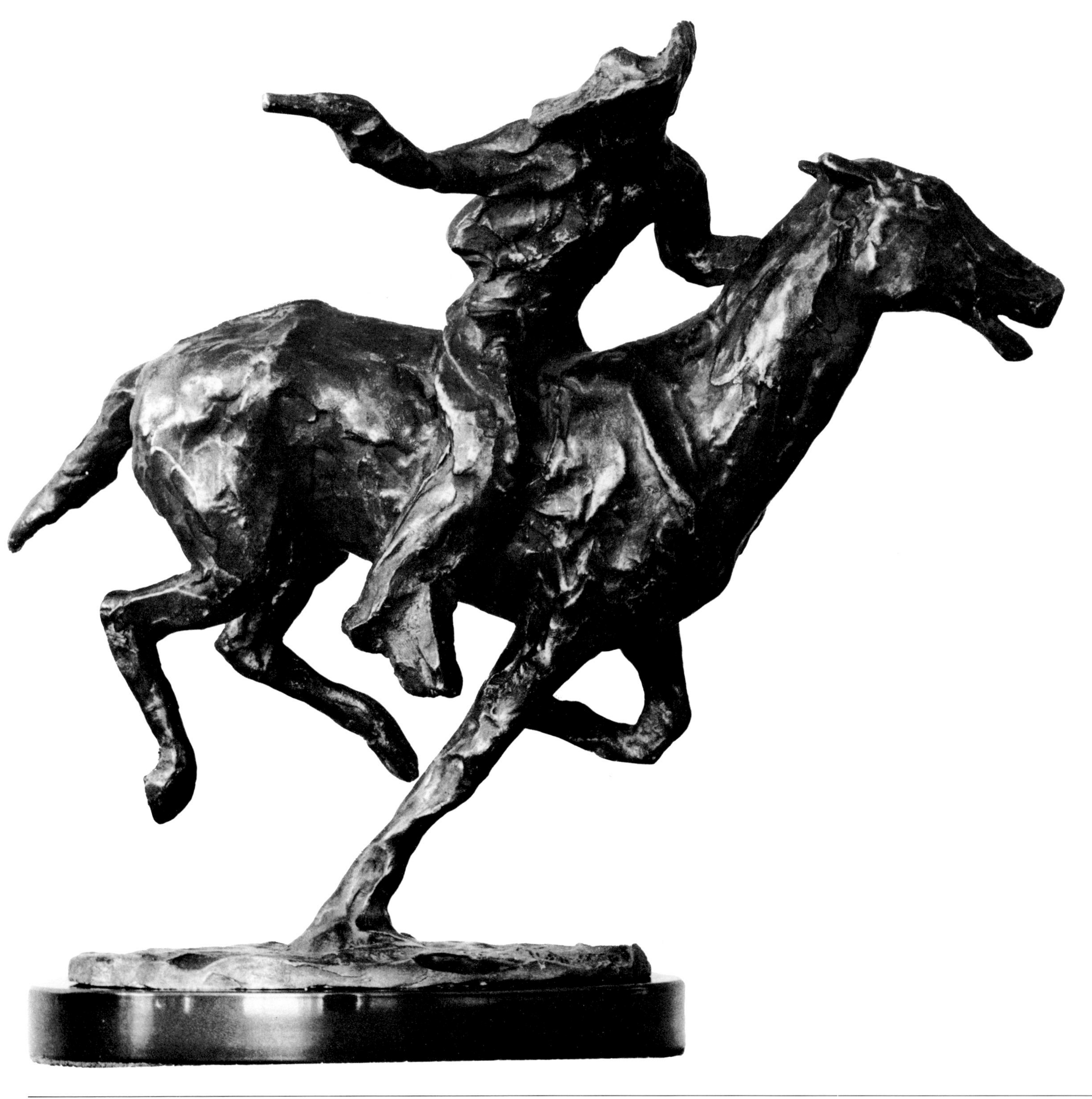

Pony Express — First Study, bronze,
10½ x 12 x 6½ ", 1963
Wyoming Foundry Studios

Pony Express, polychrome bronze,
18½ x 21 x 14", 1967
Wyoming Foundry Studios

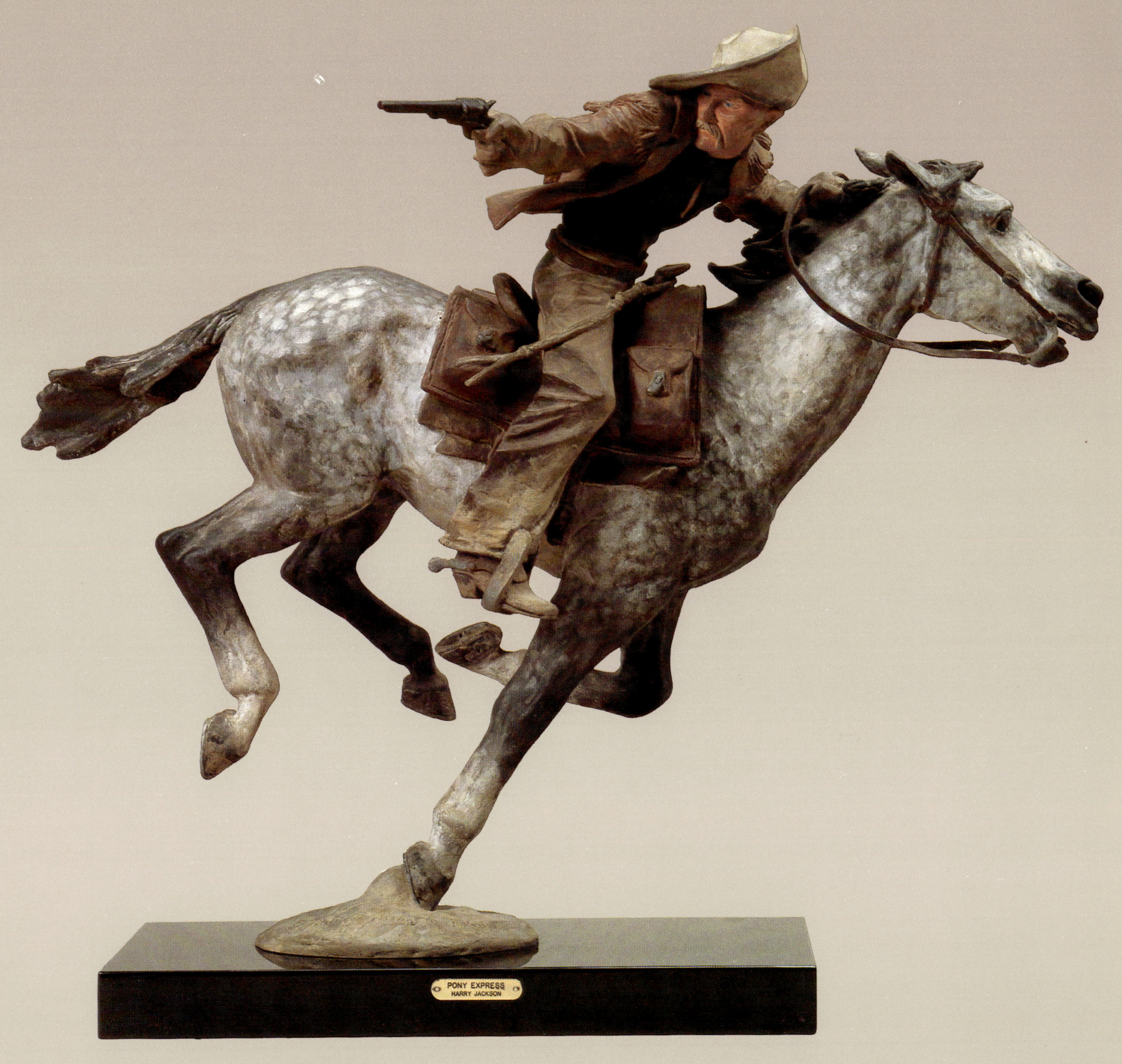

PONY EXPRESS
HARRY JACKSON

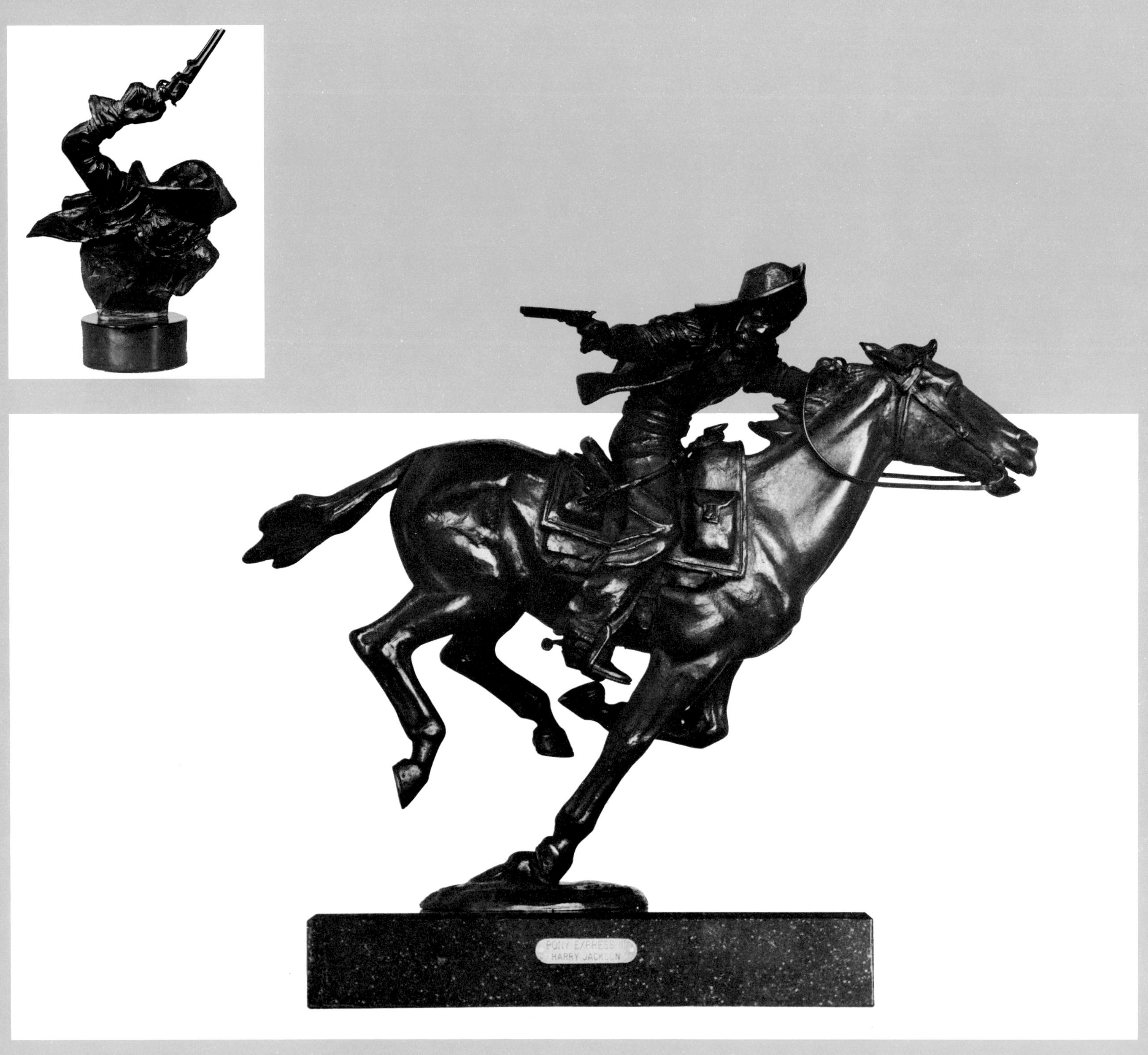

Pony Express Rider, Bust, bronze,
11 x 7 x 7½", 1972
Wyoming Foundry Studios

Pony Express III, bronze,
8½ x 9½ x 6¼", 1978
Wyoming Foundry Studios

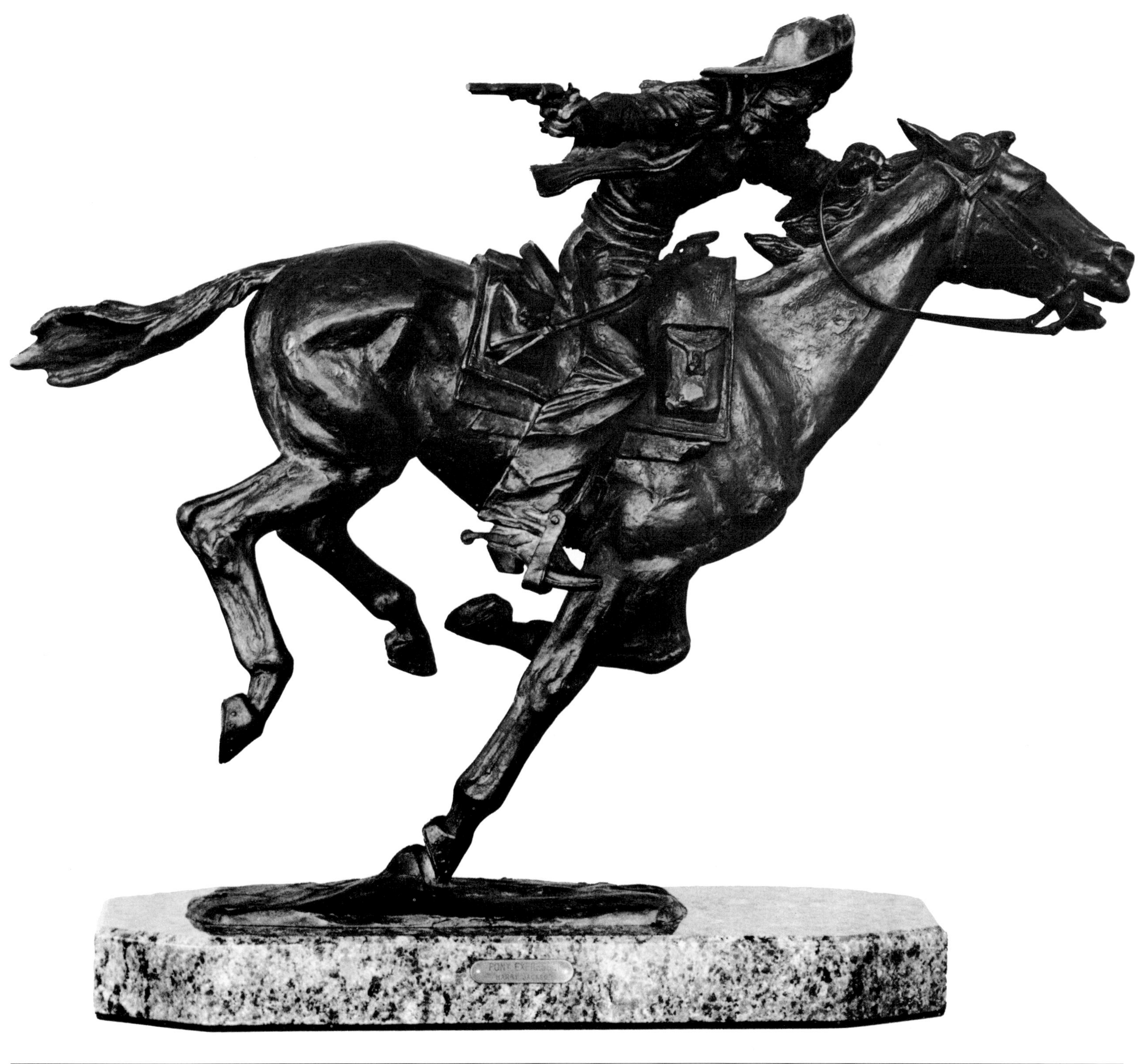

Pony Express II, bronze,
13½ x 16⅛ x 10½ ", 1980
Wyoming Foundry Studios

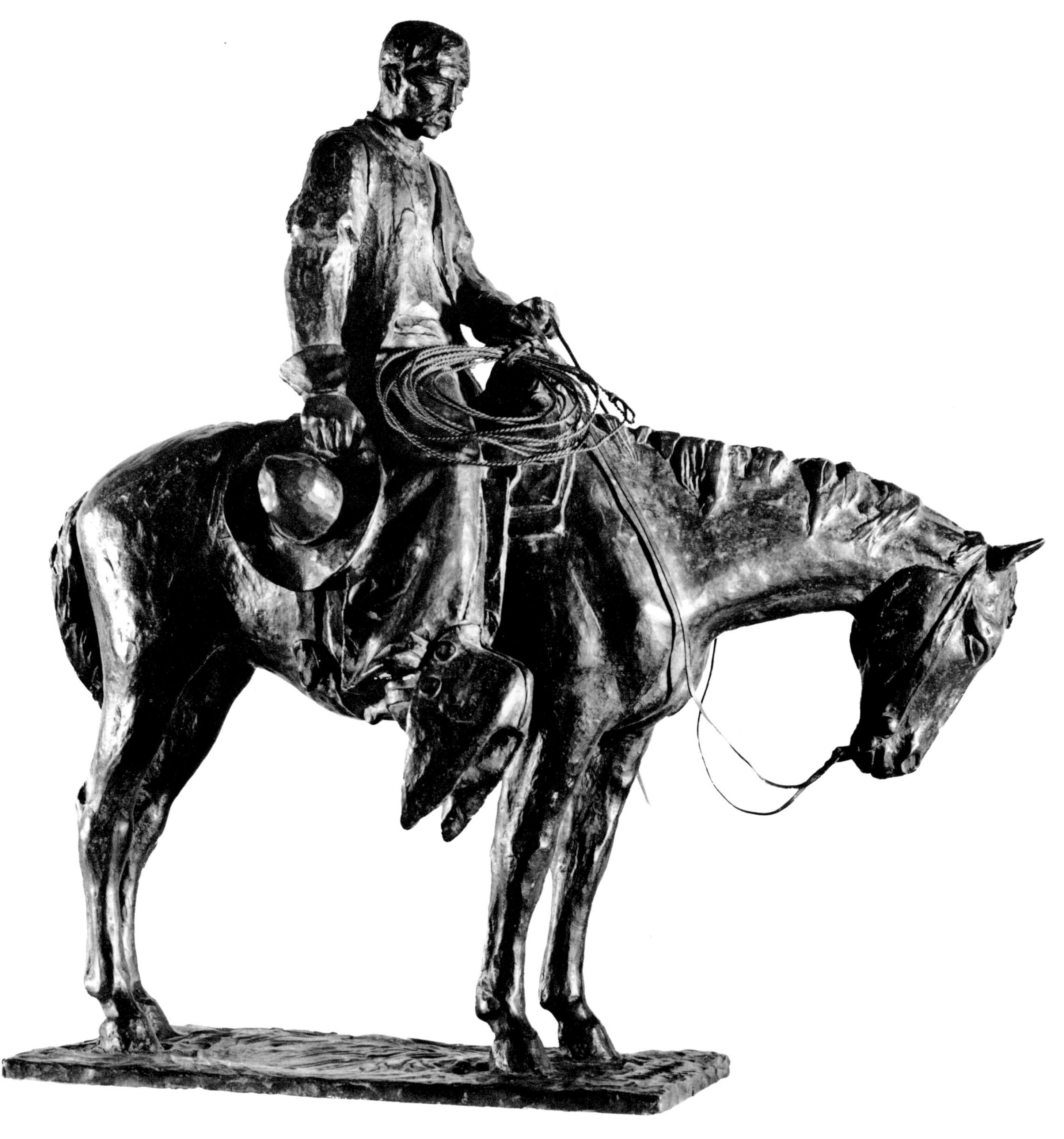

Cowboy Meditation, bronze,
22 x 20½ x 9″, 1964
Buffalo Bill Historical Center

. . . the patinaed bronze, express(es)
individually the profound grief that
makes this a classic achievement
of Western art.

Frank Getlein
Harry Jackson, 1969

Cowboy Meditation,
polychrome bronze,
22 x 20½ x 9″, 1964
Wyoming Foundry Studios

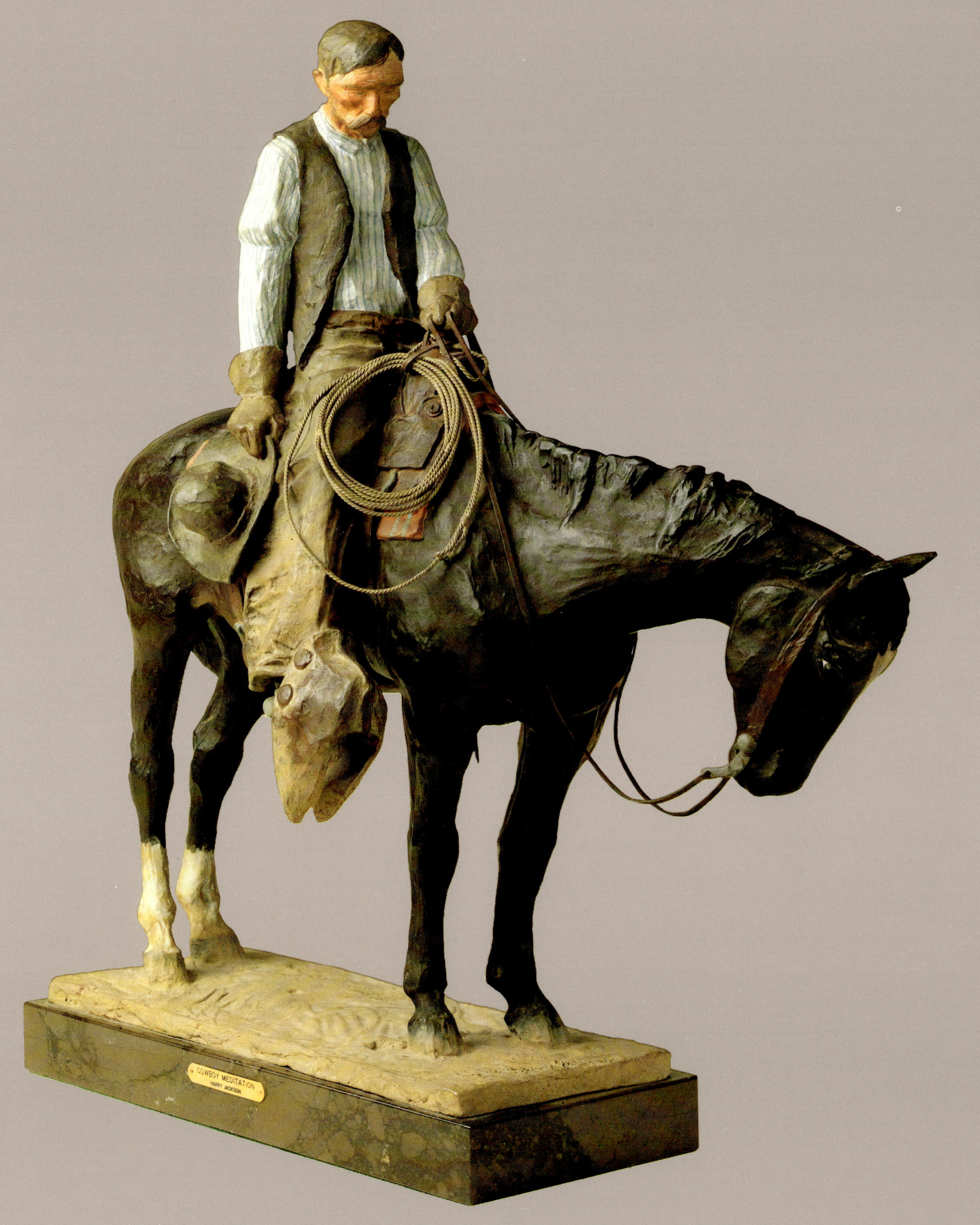
COWBOY MEDITATION
HARRY JACKSON

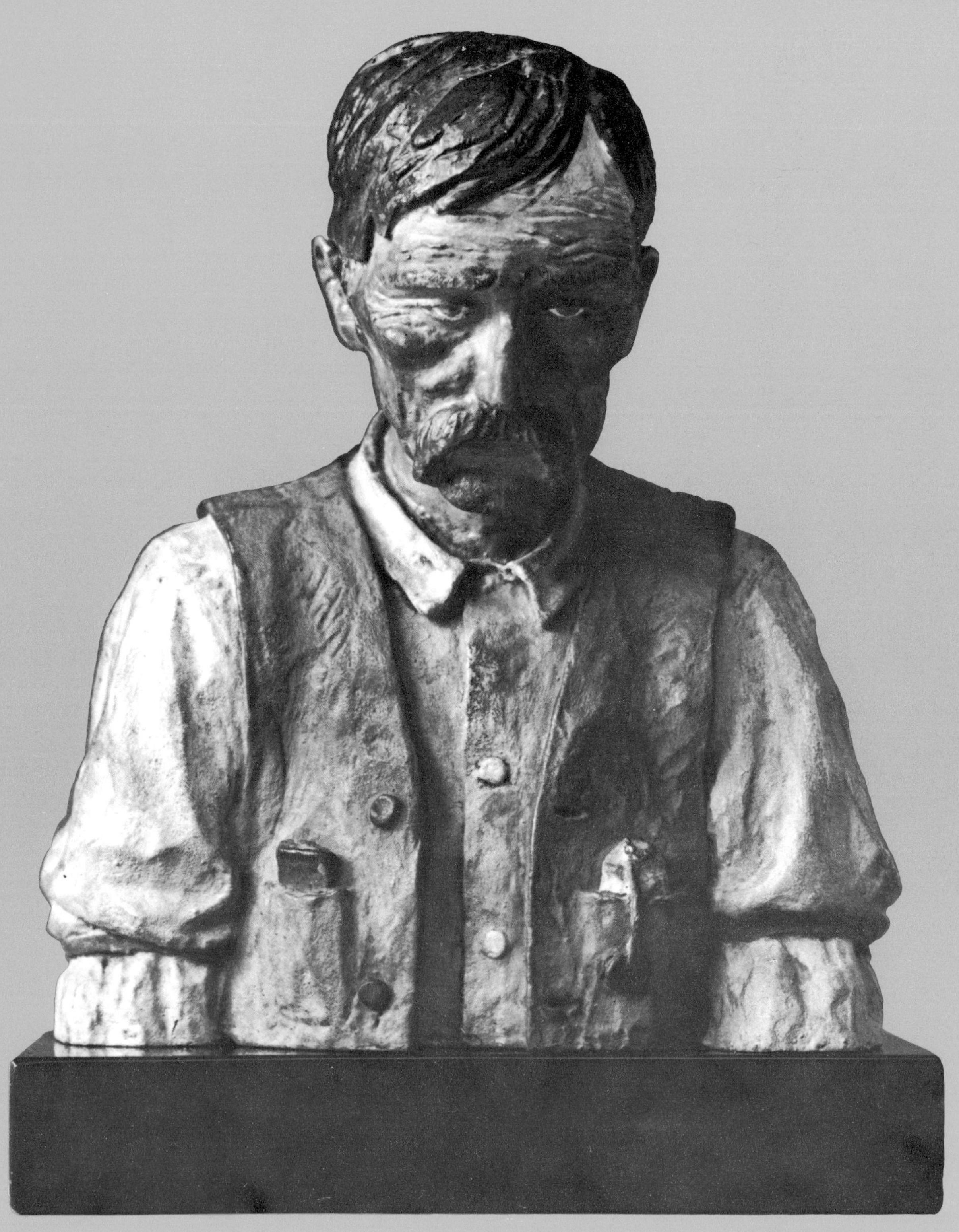

Old Timer, polychrome bronze,
6 x 4¼ x 2¾", 1969
Wyoming Foundry Studios

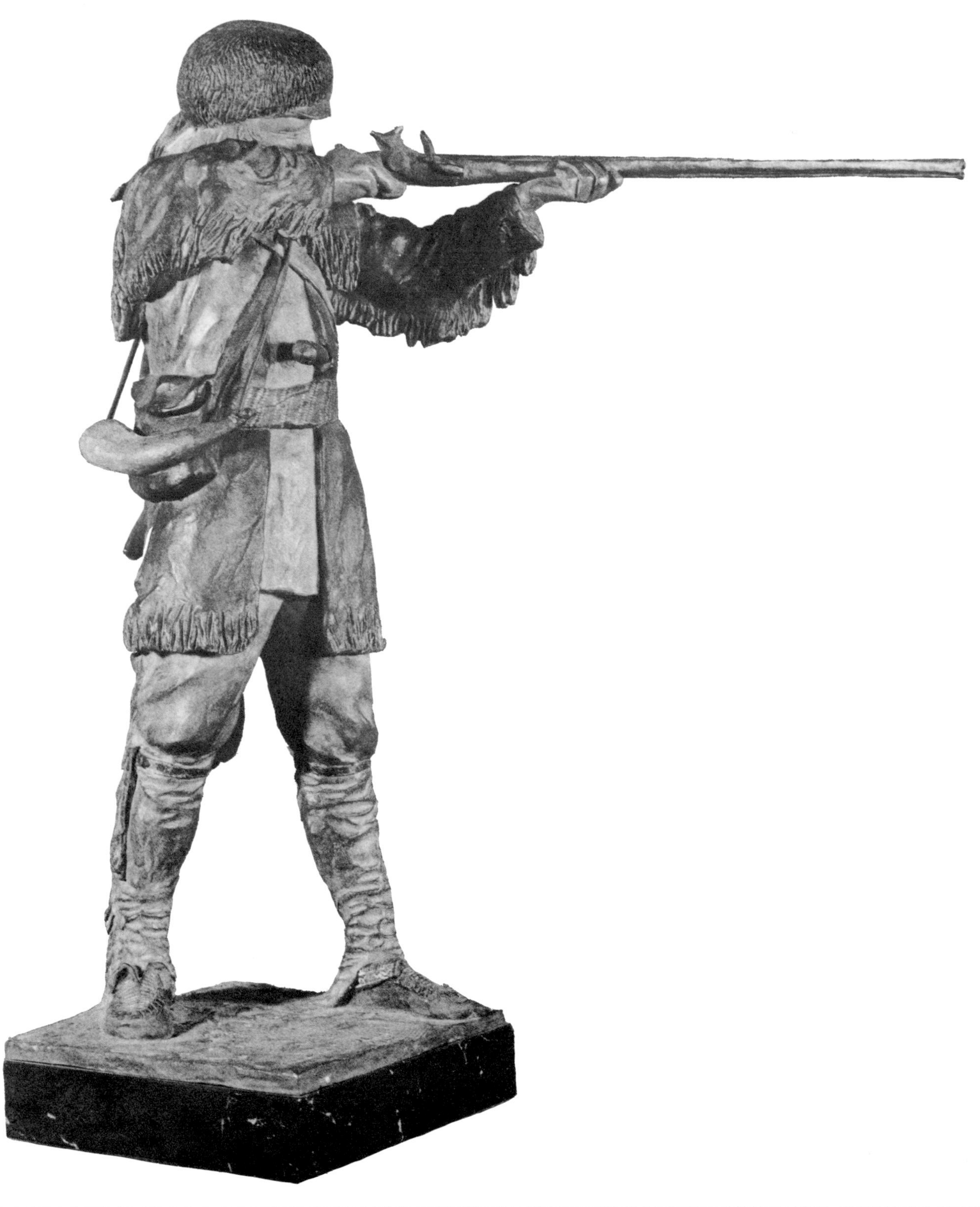

Frontiersman, polychrome bronze,
20 x 18 x 10″, 1965
Wyoming Foundry Studios

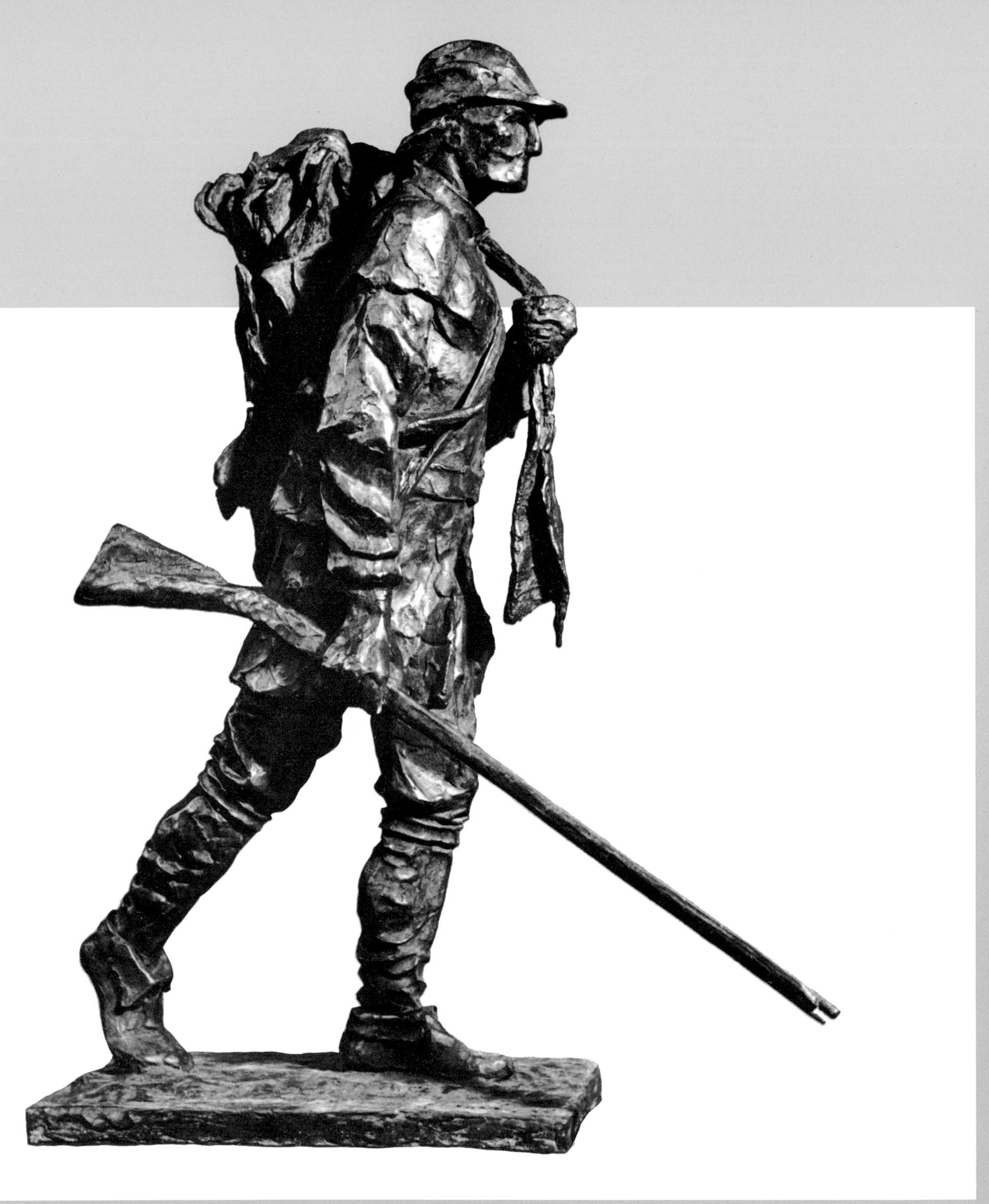

Trapper Study, bronze,
20 x 14¾ x 8¾″, 1968
Wyoming Foundry Studios

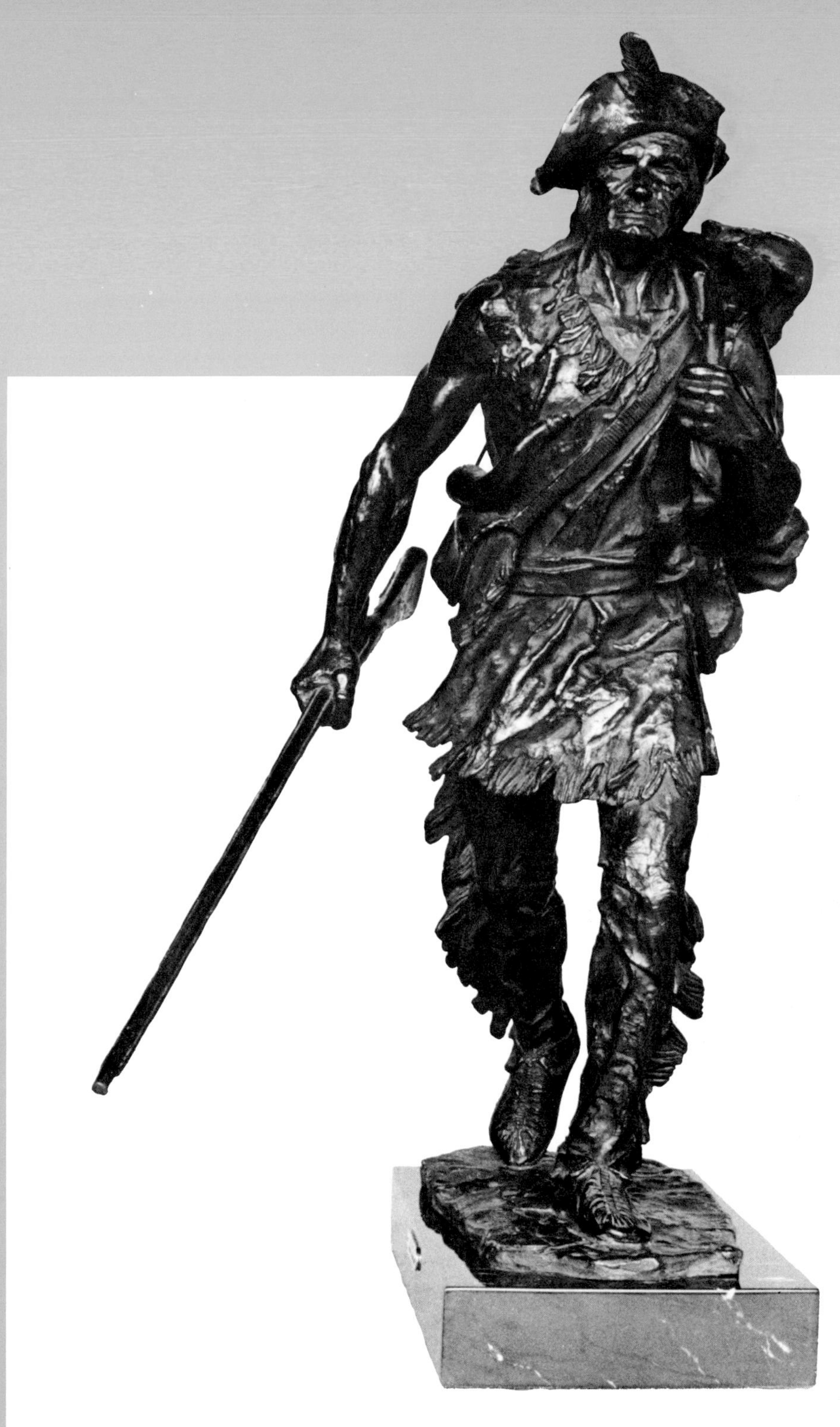

Trapper, bronze,
15 x 20¾ x 11½″, 1970
Wyoming Foundry Studios

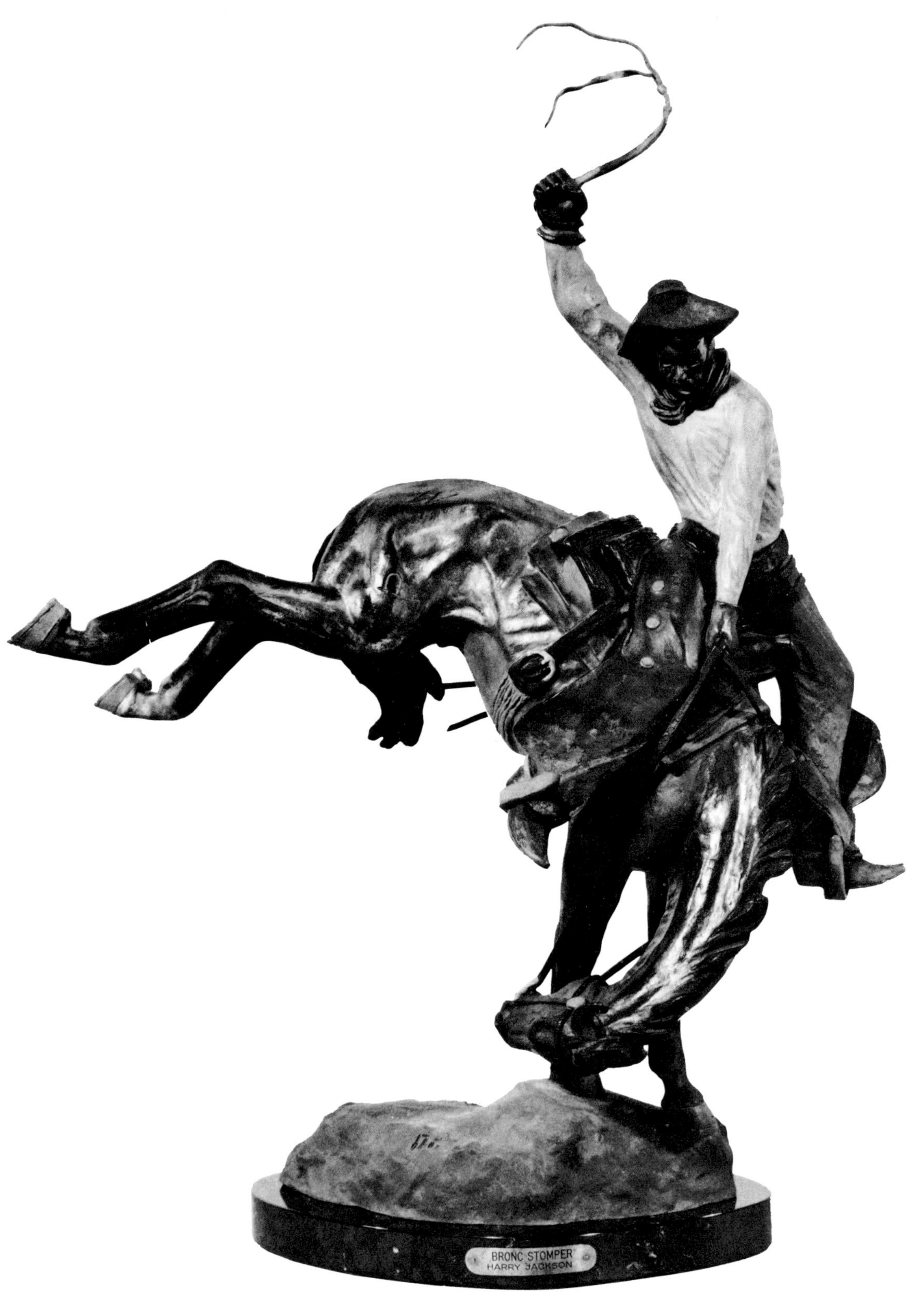

Bronc Stomper,
polychrome bronze,
17 x 18½ x 5½ ", 1968
Wyoming Foundry Studios

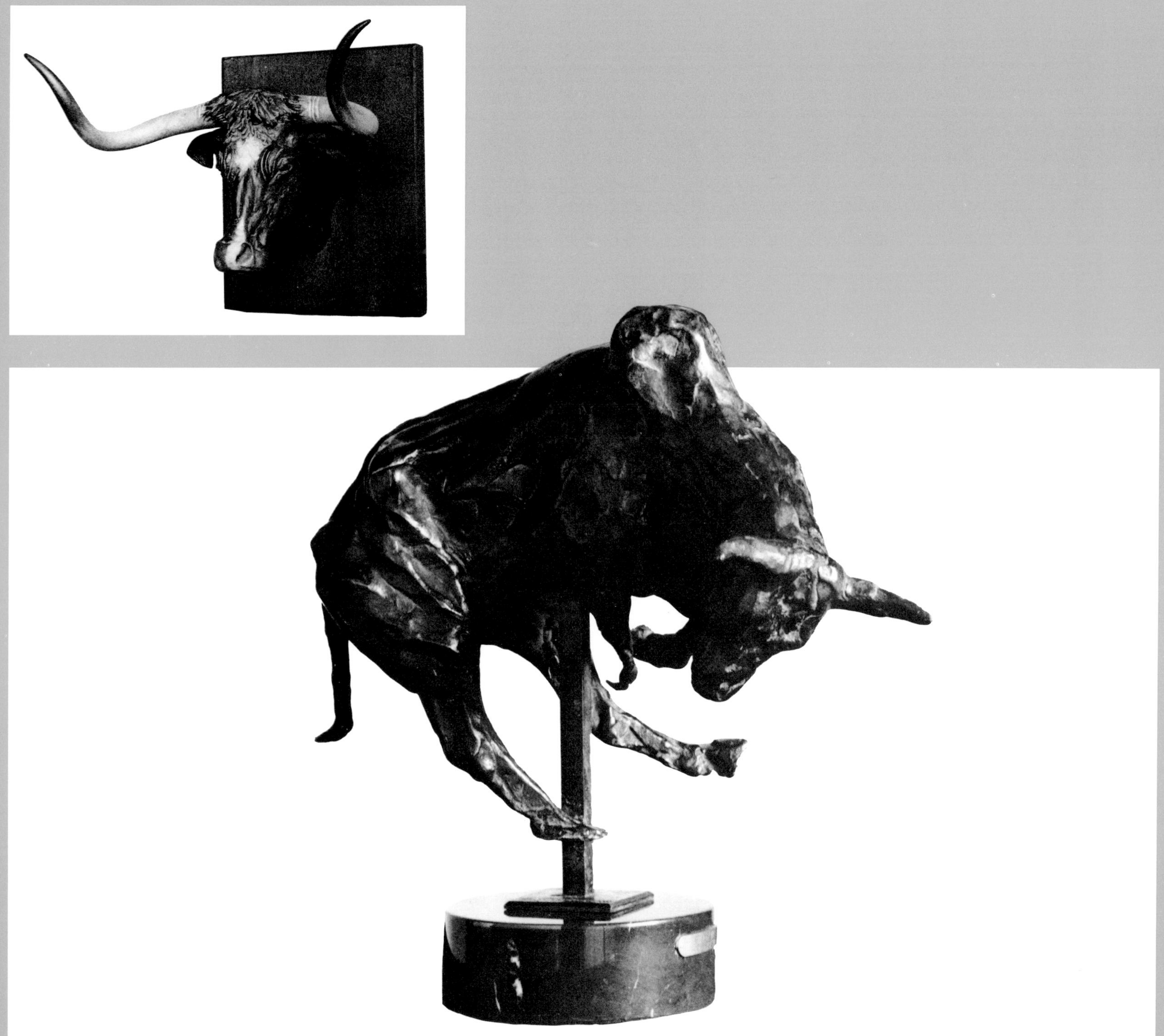

Longhorn, polychrome bronze,
7 x 8½ x 6¾", 1968
Wyoming Foundry Studios

Bull Study, bronze,
11½ x 11½ x 8", 1970
Wyoming Foundry Studios

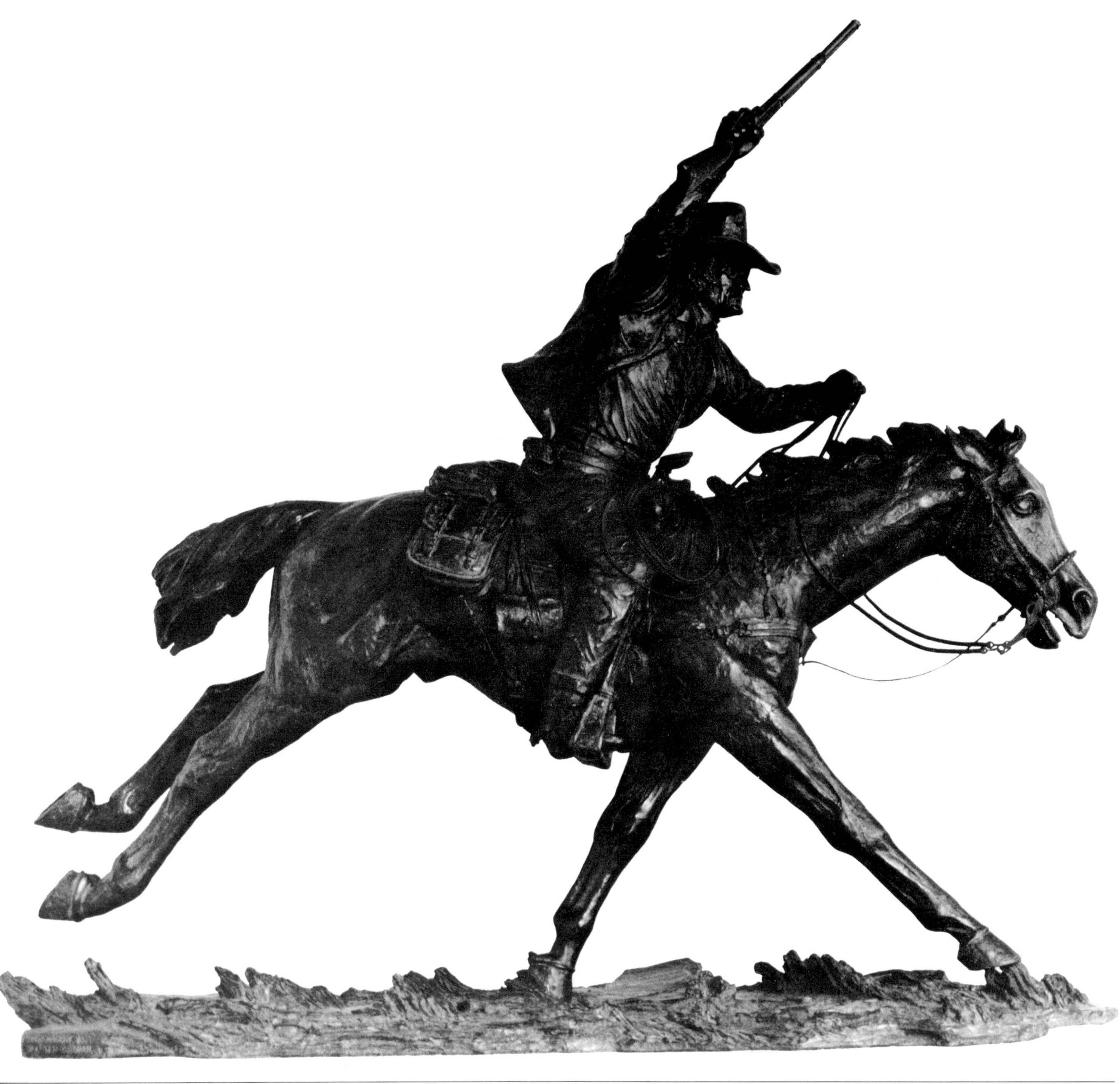

The Marshall, bronze,
29 x 33 x 13", 1970
Wyoming Foundry Studios

The Marshall II, bronze,
16-15/32 x 17-15/16 x 5⅞", 1979
Wyoming Foundry Studios

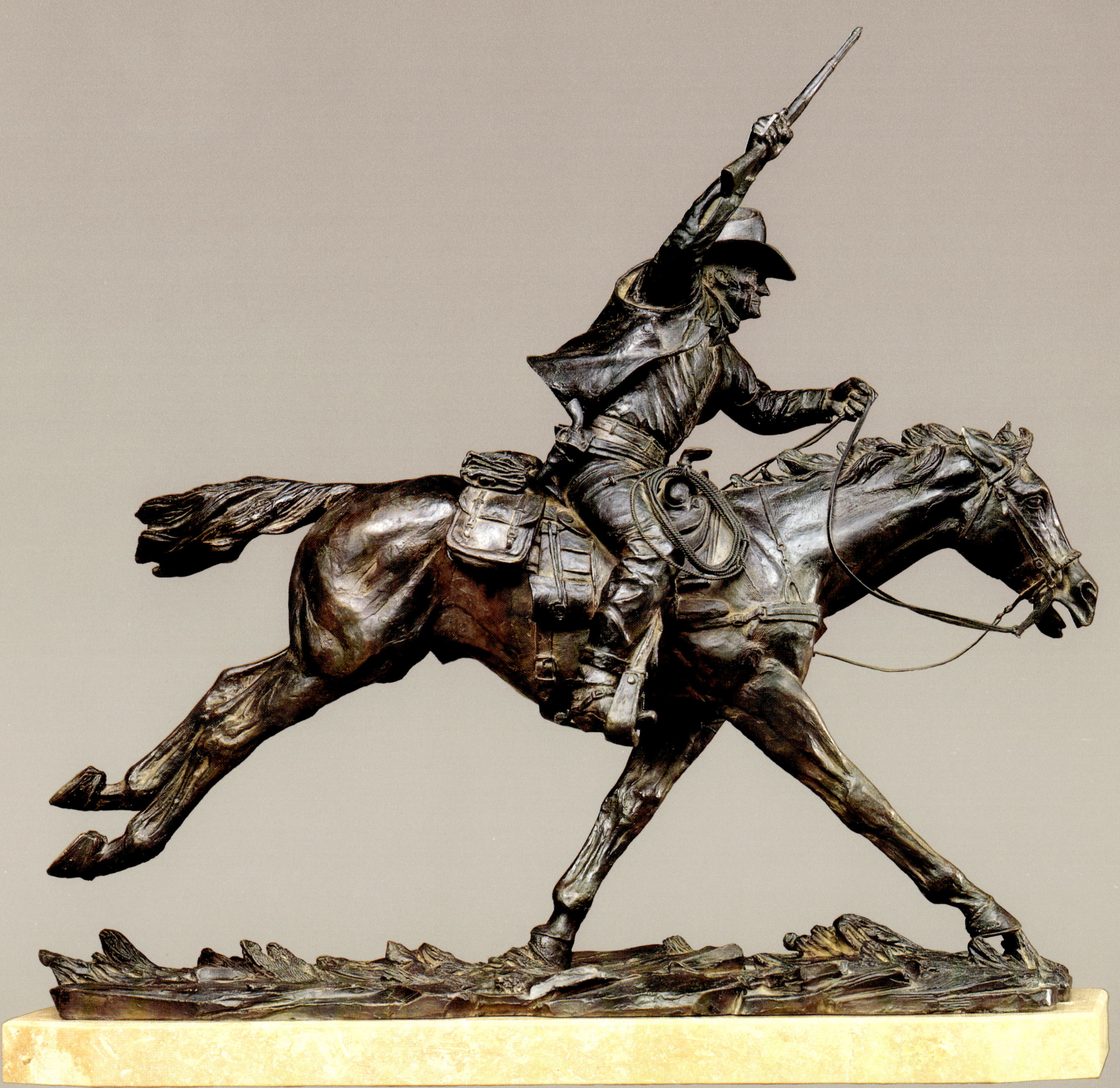

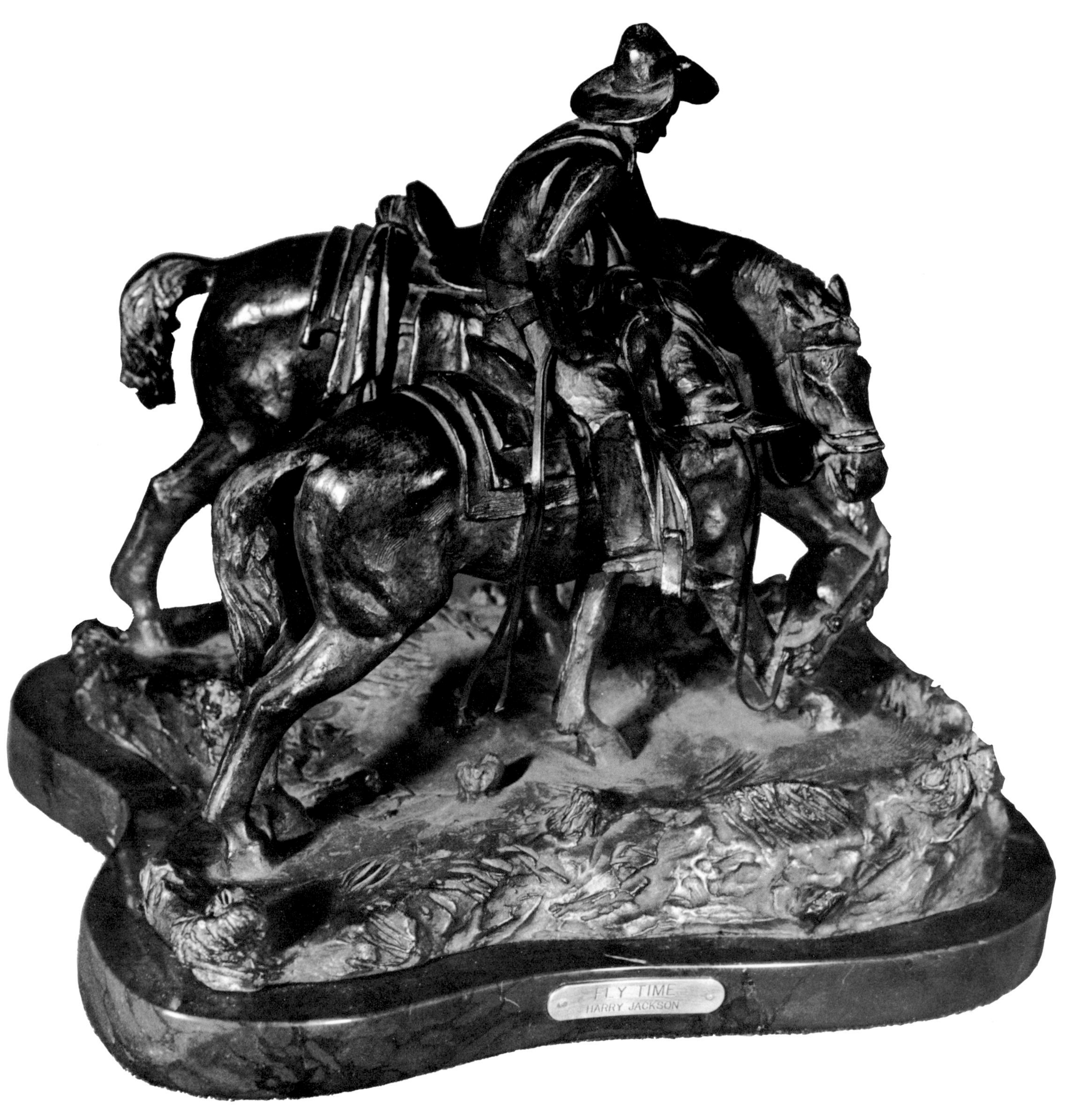

Fly Time, bronze,
9¼ x 9½ x 8″, 1969
Wyoming Foundry Studios

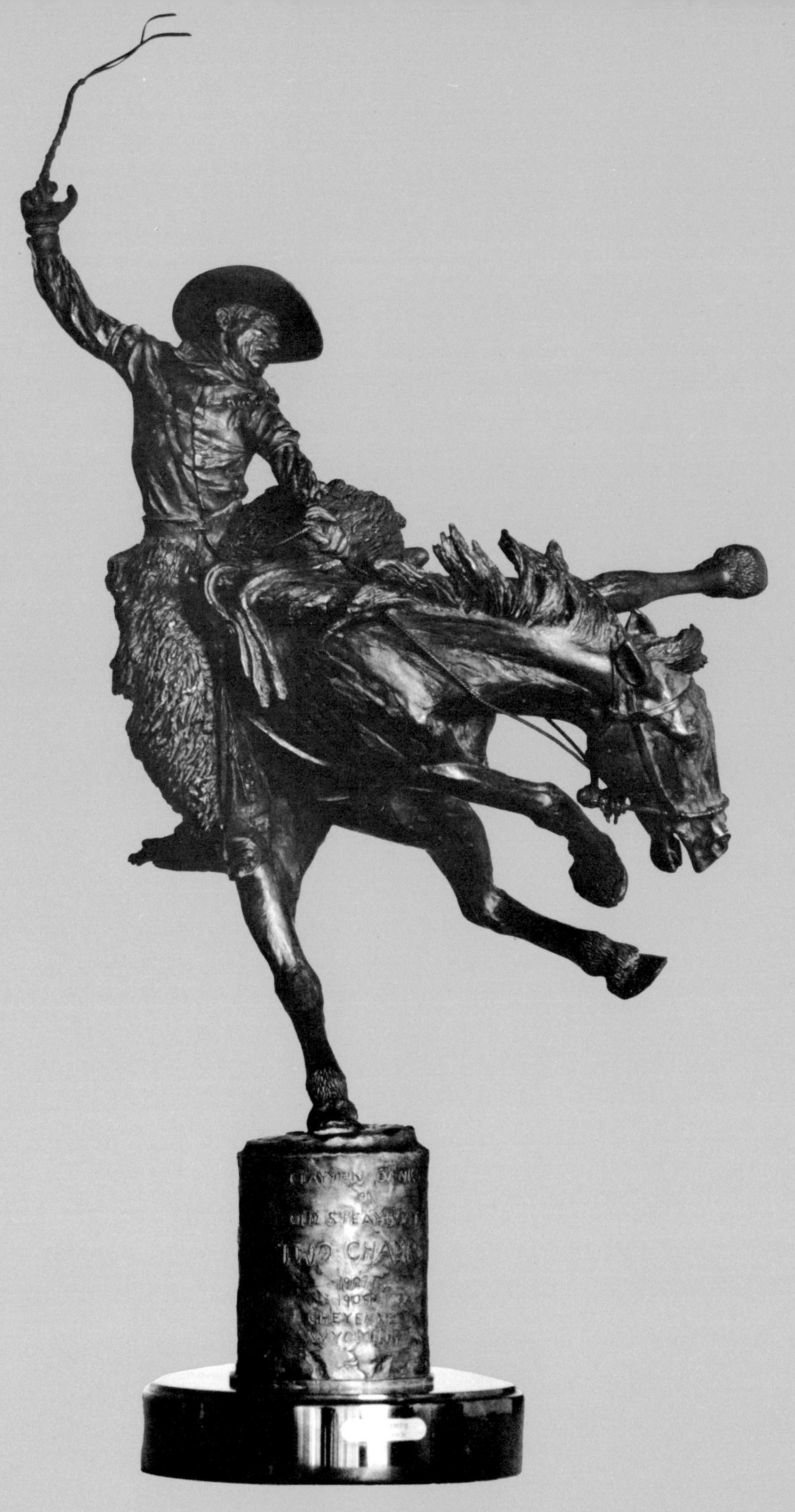

Two Champs, bronze,
30 x 19 x 15″, 1974
Wyoming Foundry Studios

Harry's bronze catches all the
rawhide, bone, muscle, leather,
denim and sweat of the West.

John Wayne
*Harry Jackson The Glory
of the Old West,* 1979

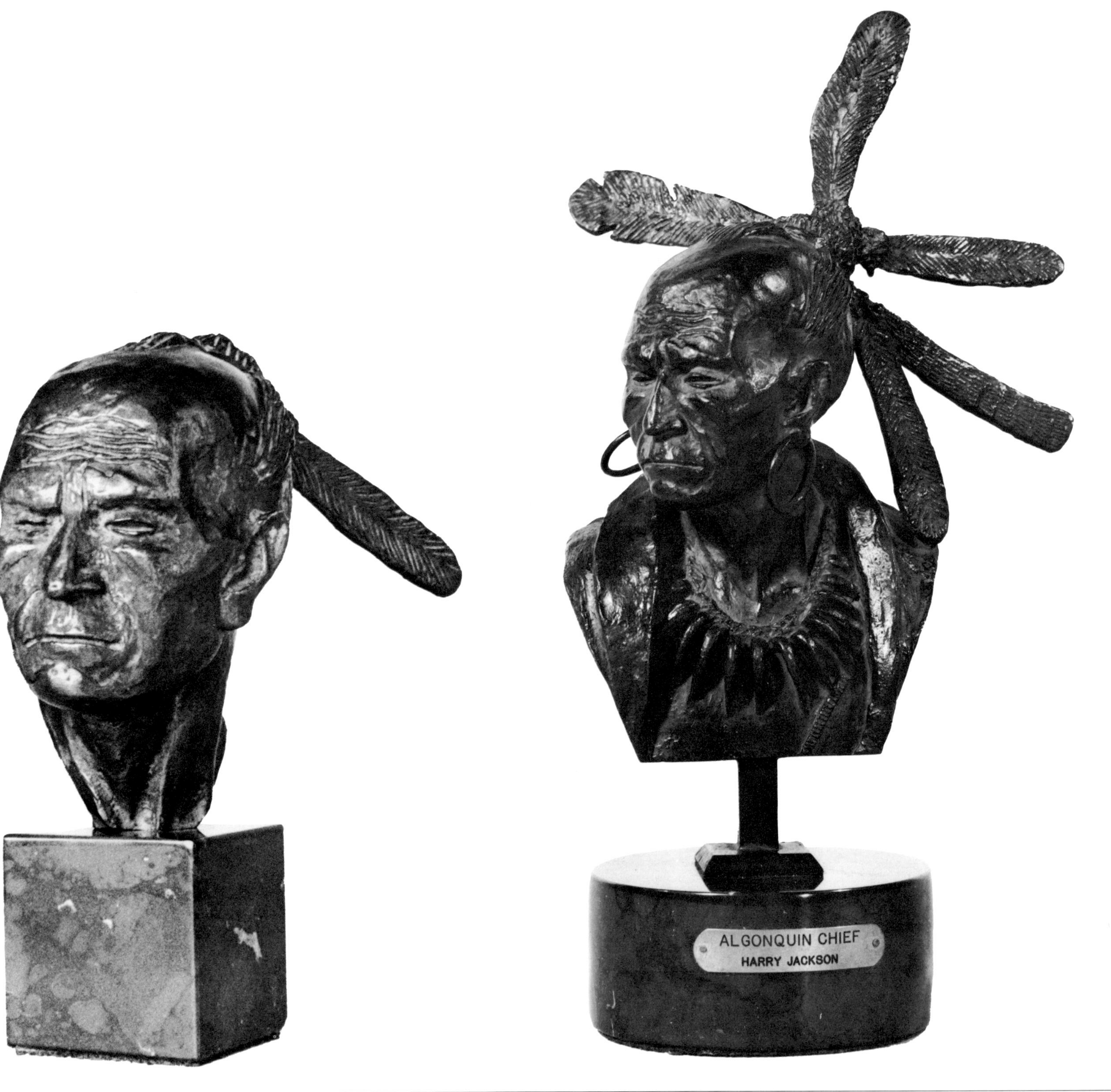

One Feather, bronze,
5½ x 3 x 4¾", 1971
Wyoming Foundry Studios

Algonquin Chief, Bust, bronze,
5½ x 10½ x 5¾", 1971
Wyoming Foundry Studios

Iroquois Guide,
polychrome bronze,
19½ x 13½ x 10", 1967
Wyoming Foundry Studios

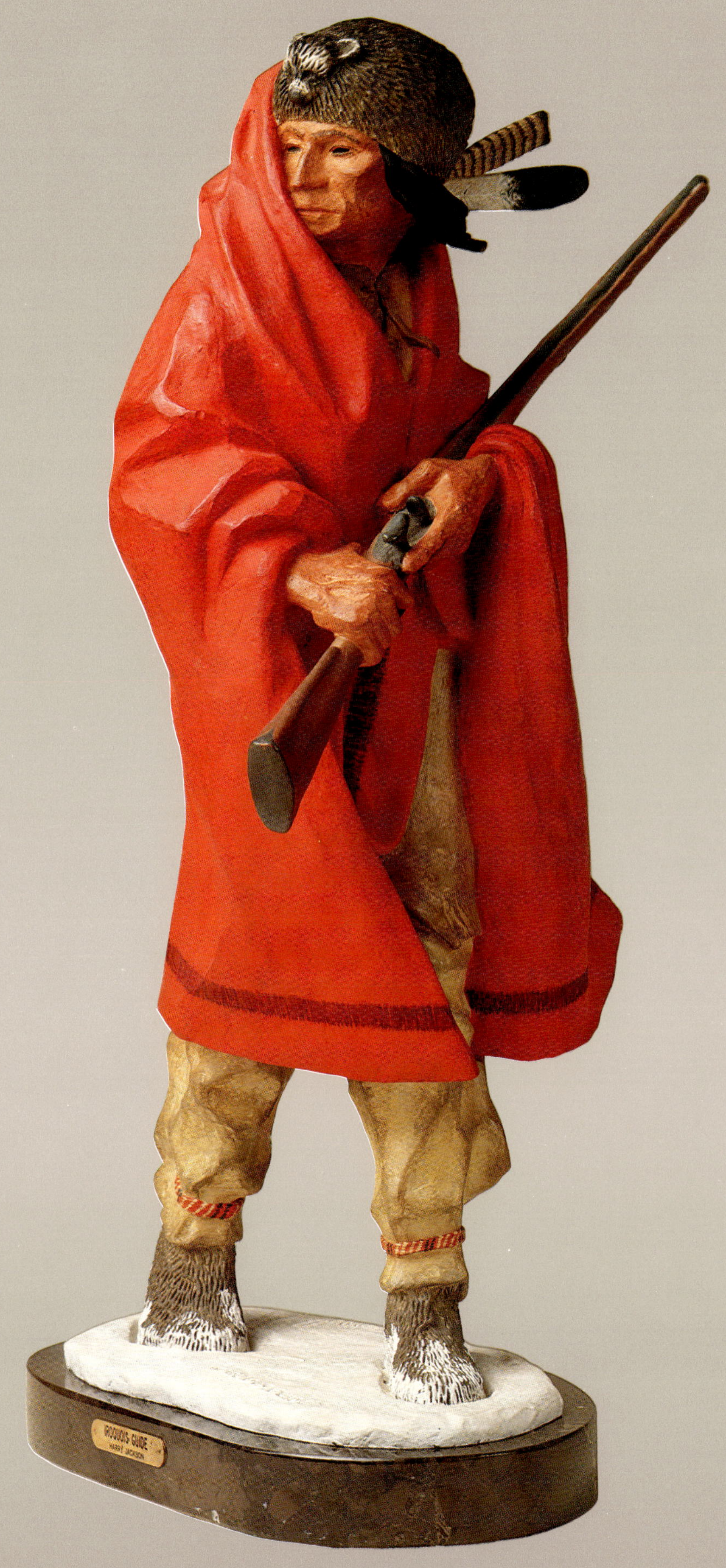

IROQUOIS GUIDE
HARRY JACKSON

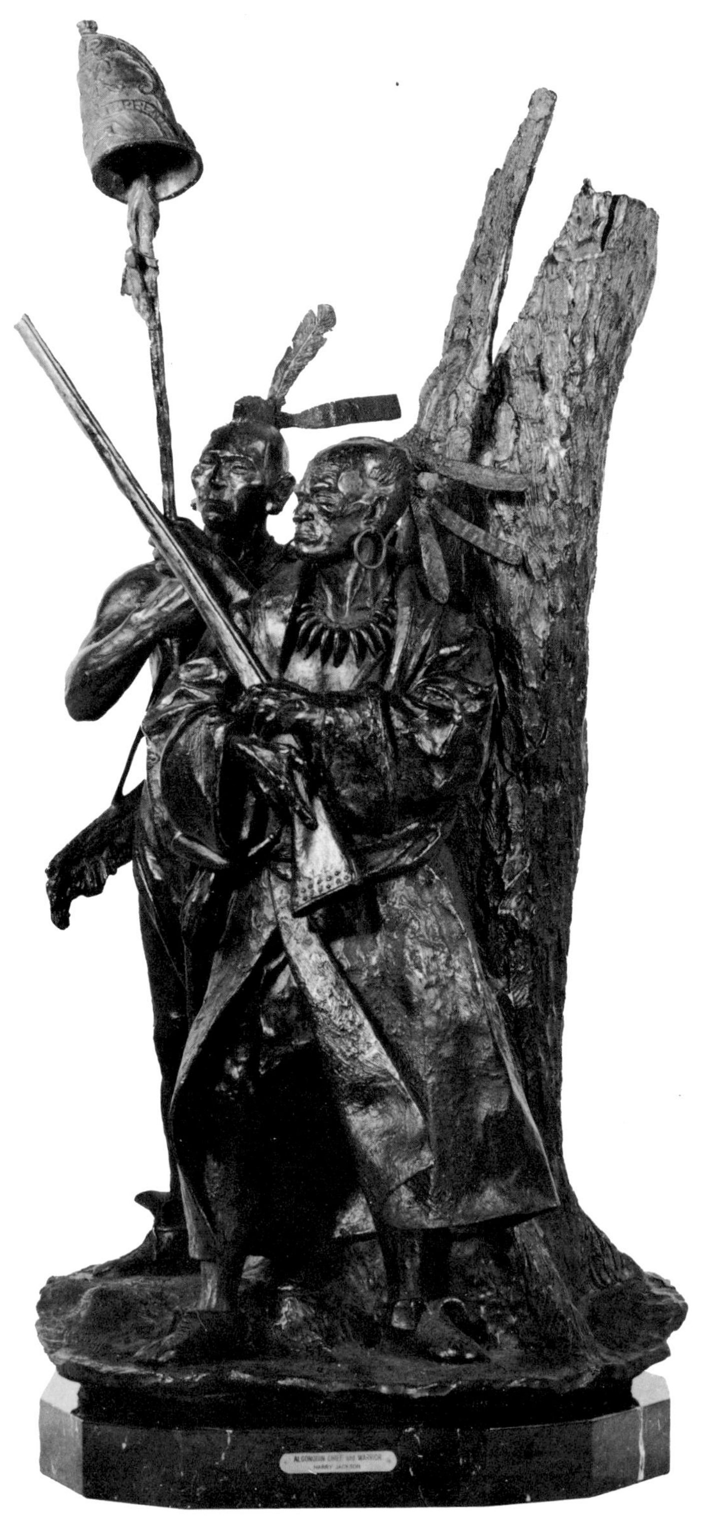

Algonquin Chief and Warrior,
bronze, 14½ x 31⅝ x 13¾", 1971
Wyoming Foundry Studios

Sacagawea with Packhorse,
bronze, 27¼ x 12½ x 19½", 1978
Wyoming Foundry Studios

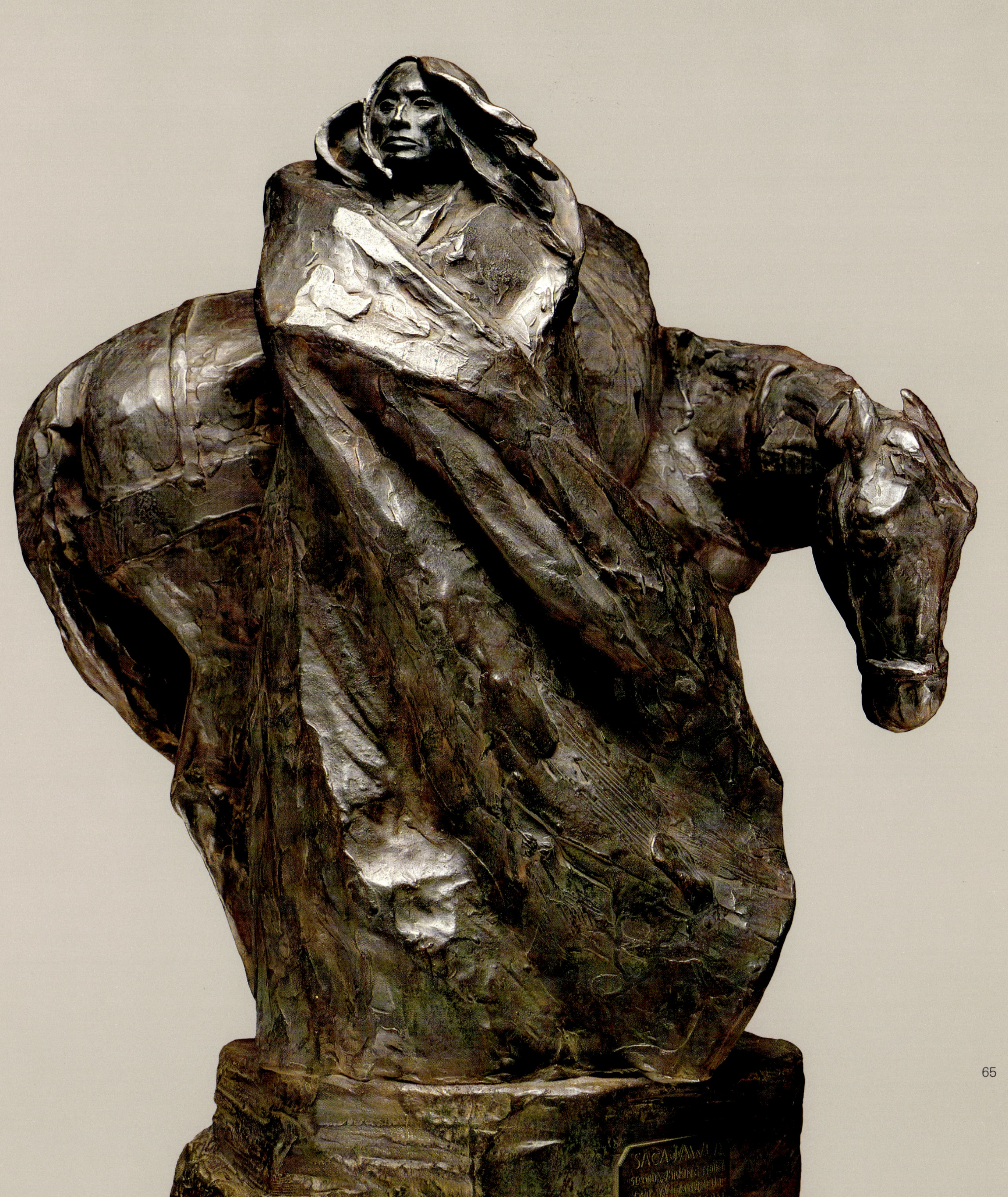

SACAJAWEA
SECOND WORKING MODEL
HARRY JACKSON

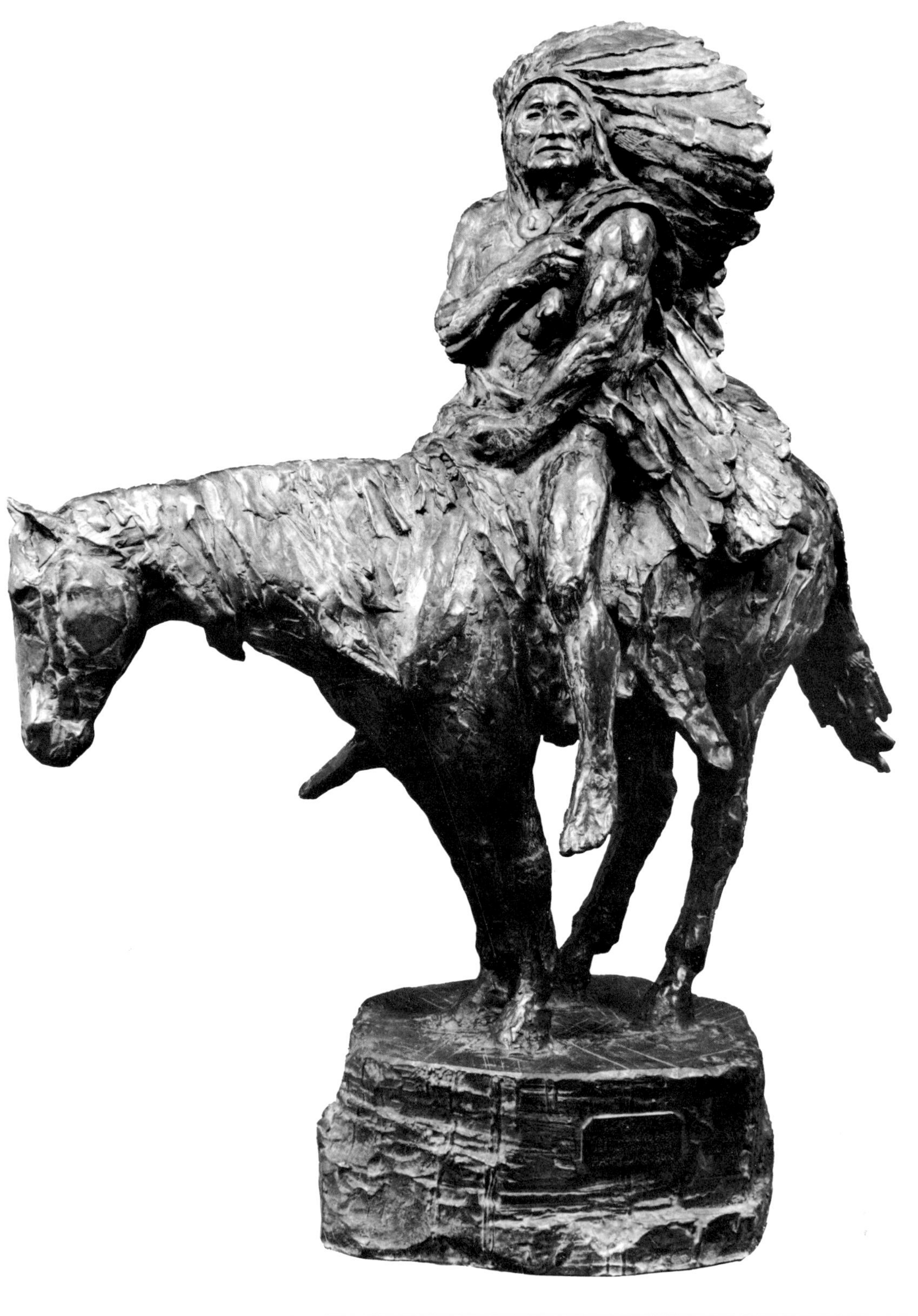

Washakie, bronze,
11½ x 12½ x 4¾″, 1978
Wyoming Foundry Studios

Sacagawea II, polychrome bronze,
18 x 8 x 6¼″, 1980
Wyoming Foundry Studios

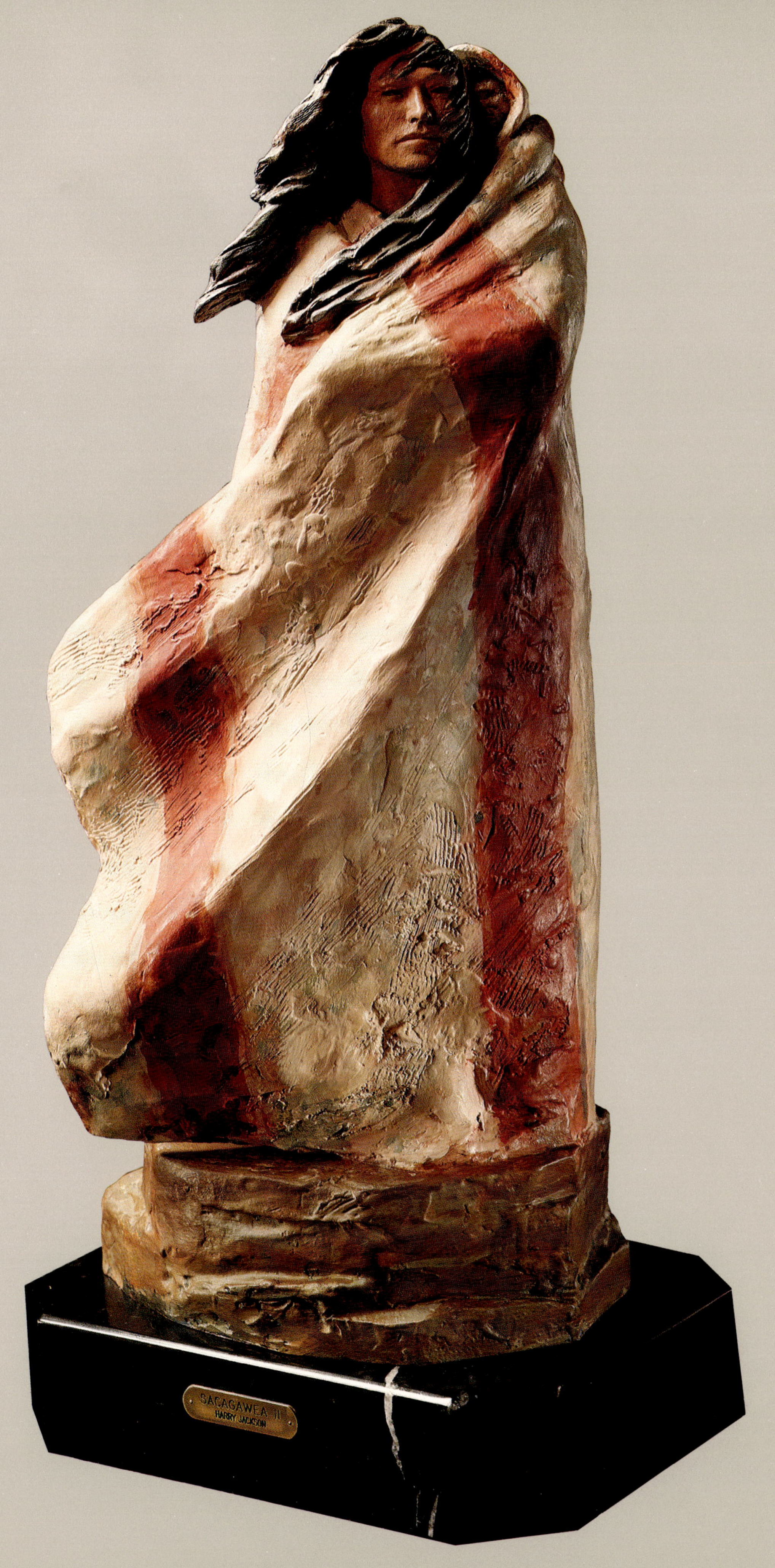
SACAGAWEA II
HARRY JACKSON

Checklist

Untitled — cowboy roping horses,
oil on canvas,
24 x 30″, 1941
Wyoming Foundry Studios

Assault, oil on canvas,
20 x 26″, 1945
Wyoming Foundry Studios

Untitled — portrait bust of
woman, oil on canvas,
22 x 18″, 1947
Wyoming Foundry Studios

Untitled — portrait bust of
woman, oil on canvas,
20 x 16″, 1946
Wyoming Foundry Studios

Untitled — Cubist still life,
oil on board,
30¼ x 25″, c. 1947
Wyoming Foundry Studios

Still Life, oil on canvas,
12 x 16″, 1948
Wyoming Foundry Studios

Grace Hartigan, oil on canvas,
36 x 60″, 1949
Wyoming Foundry Studios

Collage, mixed media,
33 x 24″, 1949
Wyoming Foundry Studios

Fiesta, oil on canvas,
40 x 40″, 1950
Karen and Emmanuel Ghent

Family, oil on canvas,
92½ x 134″, 1953
Wyoming Foundry Studios

The Italian Bar, oil on canvas,
7 x 9′, 1956
Wyoming Foundry Studios

The Trail Driver, oil on canvas,
84¼ x 44″, 1956
Buffalo Bill Historical Center

The Poet, Robert Lax,
oil on canvas,
78½ x 35½″, 1962
Wyoming Foundry Studios

Portrait of a Physician,
oil on canvas,
23¾ x 21¾″, 1962
Dr. Adrian W. Zorgniotti

Frank Lamb, oil on canvas,
19¼ x 23″, 1963
Mrs. Adrian W. Zorgniotti

Range Burial, oil on canvas,
10 x 21′, 1963
Buffalo Bill Historical Center

Portrait Study for Range Burial,
oil on canvas,
38¾ x 30⅞″, 1959
Mrs. Henry H.R. Coe

Looking Things Over, oil on panel,
12 x 16″, 1964
Wyoming Foundry Studios

Two *Landscape Studies,*
oil on canvas, 12 x 16″, 1964
Wyoming Foundry Studios

Four *Studies for Stampede,*
oil on canvas,
19 x 42″, 1964
Wyoming Foundry Studios

Final Study for Stampede,
egg tempera and oil on canvas,
22 x 48″, 1965
Wyoming Foundry Studios

Stampede, oil on canvas,
10 x 21′, 1965
Buffalo Bill Historical Center

Range Burial, bronze,
15 x 43 x 23″, 1958
Buffalo Bill Historical Center

Trail Boss, bronze,
8¼ x 8 x 3¼″, 1958
Wyoming Foundry Studios

Ground Roper, bronze,
10 x 5 x 4″, 1958
Wyoming Foundry Studios

Stampede, bronze,
53⅜ x 14¼ x 14¼″, 1959
Buffalo Bill Historical Center

Settin' Purty, bronze,
16 x 10¼ x 6″, 1959
Wyoming Foundry Studios

Ropin', bronze,
13½ x 17½ x 5¼″, 1959
Wyoming Foundry Studios

Long Ballad, bronze,
6 x 5 x 4″, 1959
Buffalo Bill Historical Center

Steer Roper, Hard and Fast,
bronze,
12 x 25 x 12″, 1959
Buffalo Bill Historical Center

Salty Dog, bronze,
10¼ x 5 x 4½″, 1959
Wyoming Foundry Studios

Plantin', bronze,
13 x 26½ x 12½″, 1960
Wyoming Foundry Studios

Lone Hand, bronze,
15 x 15 x 6″, 1961
Buffalo Bill Historical Center

First Saddle, bronze,
12 x 11¼ x 3¾″, 1961
Wyoming Foundry Studios

Where the Trail Forks,
polychrome bronze,
19½ x 5¾ x 5½″, 1962
Wyoming Foundry Studios

Gunsil, polychrome bronze,
18⅛ x 6¼ x 6″, 1962
Buffalo Bill Historical Center

Pony Express — First Study,
bronze,
10½ x 12 x 6½″, 1963
Wyoming Foundry Studios

Pony Express, polychrome bronze,
18½ x 21 x 14″, 1967
Wyoming Foundry Studios

*Pony Express — Unfinished
Sketch,* bronze,
10¾ x 11½ x 2¾″, 1968
Wyoming Foundry Studios

Pony Express Rider, Bust, bronze,
11 x 7 x 7½″, 1972
Wyoming Foundry Studios

Pony Express II, bronze,
13½ x 16⅛ x 10½″, 1980
Wyoming Foundry Studios

Pony Express III, bronze,
8½ x 9½ x 6¼″, 1978
Wyoming Foundry Studios

Cowboy Meditation,
polychrome bronze,
22 x 20½ x 9″, 1964
Wyoming Foundry Studios

Cowboy Meditation, bronze,
22 x 20½ x 9″, 1964
Buffalo Bill Historical Center

Frontiersman, polychrome bronze,
20 x 18 x 10″, 1965
Wyoming Foundry Studios

Iroquois Guide,
polychrome bronze,
19½ x 13½ x 10″, 1967
Wyoming Foundry Studios

Trapper Study, bronze,
20 x 14¾ x 8¾″, 1968
Wyoming Foundry Studios

Trapper, bronze,
15 x 20¾ x 11½″, 1970
Wyoming Foundry Studios

Bronc Stomper,
polychrome bronze,
17 x 18½ x 5½″, 1968
Wyoming Foundry Studios

Longhorn, polychrome bronze,
7 x 8½ x 6¾″, 1968
Wyoming Foundry Studios

Fly Time, bronze,
9¼ x 9½ x 8″, 1969
Wyoming Foundry Studios

Old Timer, polychrome bronze,
6 x 4¼ x 2¾″, 1969
Wyoming Foundry Studios

The Marshall, bronze,
29 x 33 x 13″, 1970
Wyoming Foundry Studios

The Marshall II, bronze,
16-15/32 x 17-15/16 x 5⅞″, 1979
Wyoming Foundry Studios

Bull Study, bronze,
11½ x 11½ x 8″, 1970
Wyoming Foundry Studios

Algonquin Chief and Warrior,
bronze,
14½ x 31⅝ x 13¾″, 1971
Wyoming Foundry Studios

One Feather, bronze,
5½ x 3 x 4¾″, 1971
Wyoming Foundry Studios

Algonquin Chief, Bust, bronze,
5½ x 10½ x 5¾″, 1971
Wyoming Foundry Studios

Washakie, bronze,
11½ x 12½ x 4¾″, 1978
Wyoming Foundry Studios

Sacagawea with Packhorse,
bronze,
27¼ x 12½ x 19½″, 1978
Wyoming Foundry Studios

Two Champs, bronze,
30 x 19 x 15″, 1974
Wyoming Foundry Studios

Ol Sabertooth, bronze,
10 x 6½ x 6¼″, 1980
Wyoming Foundry Studios

Sacagawea II, polychrome bronze,
18 x 8 x 6¼″, 1980
Wyoming Foundry Studios

Selected Bibliography

Amaya, Mario. "Harry Jackson, Sculptor of the American West," *The Connoisseur* (September, 1979), 28-37.

Aubuchon, Ruth. "Two Champs for the Queen," *In Wyoming* (February/March, 1977), 14-17.

Barber, Margery Torrey. "The Artist in Control of His Destiny: Harry Jackson," *Southwest Art* (April, 1978), 43-47, 123-125.

Butler, William. "Harry Jackson: Sculptor of the American West Earns Top Success Doing Things His Own Way," *The Gilcrease* (October, 1980), 2-14.

Getlein, Frank. *Harry Jackson.* New York: Kennedy Galleries, Inc., 1969.

————————— "The Range Burial a Monumental Canvas," *American Artist* (November, 1965), 60-64, 75-78.

Goddard, Donald. "The Challenge of Public Sculpture: Harry Jackson's Monument to *Sacagawea*," *The Connoisseur* (October, 1980), 110.

————————— "Sculptor Harry Jackson's Sacagawea," *The American West* (March/April, 1980), 14-15, 56.

Harry Jackson: Western Bronzes. New York: Kennedy Galleries, Inc., Winter 1965.

Jackson, Harry. *Lost Wax Bronze Casting.* Flagstaff, Arizona: Northland Press, 1972; reprinted, New York: Van Nostrand Reinhold Company, 1979.

Linn, Phyllis. "Bronze Rush Back to a Golden West," *Classic* (February/March, 1979), 72-75.

Lowd, David G. "Death on the Range," *American Heritage* (October, 1967), 48, 83.

Montana Post. "Moving Range Burial Depiction Brings Forth Full Talents of Artist Harry Jackson," (June, 1964), 2-3.

Myers, Fred A. *Harry Jackson at Gilcrease.* Tulsa, Oklahoma: Thomas Gilcrease Museum Association, 1980.

Myers, Lee. "Just Wild About Harry." *Wyoming News* (July, 1979), 8-11.

Pointer, Larry and Goddard, Donald. *Harry Jackson.* New York: Harry N. Abrams, Inc., 1981.

Seiberling, Dorothy. "Painter Striving to Find Himself." *Life* (July 9, 1956).

Time. "Go West Again, Young Man," (May 30, 1960), 61.

Ward, Angus. "The Old West Lives in Bronze." *Western's World* (January/February, 1974), 28-31.

Wilson, Janet. "Celebrating the American West with Harry Jackson," *Artnews* (December, 1978), 58-61.

Design: James Rowley Associates, Inc., Denver, Colorado   Printing: The Pressworks, Denver, Colorado